WORK MAN SHIP

LIVING, LOVING AND LEADING AS A CHRISTIAN MAN

BY FRED J. PARRY

WorkManShip: Living, Loving and Leading As A Christian Man

Published by
Carriage House Publishers

Library of Congress Control Number: 2025902511
Paperback ISBN: 979-8-9925086-1-1
Cover Design: Michelle Drexler
Interior Design: Carolyn Preul
Copy Editor: Sandy Selby
Proofreader: Samuel P. Doherty
Printed in the United States of America

To the men who walked alongside me continually encouraging me to become the best version of myself long before I knew the real Jesus. Your patience, persistence and gentleness will one day be rewarded. Of that, I am sure.

Thank You!
FJP

What's In A Name?

> *"For we are his workmanship, created in Christ Jesus for good works, which God prepared beforehand, that we should walk in them."* EPHESIANS 2:10 ESV

Because each one of us is God's workmanship, we have the distinction of being beautifully crafted and designed with a purpose made perfect by the Creator. We have been hewn in God's image for good works and uniquely equipped to fulfill specific roles and responsibilities in this world. We can rejoice that we have been placed on this earth, at this time, for a very important reason. Because of that, let us feel empowered and encouraged to live authentically, using our gifts and talents to make a positive impact while glorifying our God in all that we do. Amen.

TABLE OF CONTENTS

INTRODUCTION

Tough Conversations

When my sons were young and suffering from a high temperature, I was grateful for the bubble gum flavoring the pharmacists added to make their medicine taste better. You, however, are a grown man and I'm not going to sugarcoat it for you. You are exhausted, frustrated, irritable and soul-sick. You'll be relieved to know there is a cure available, but I must be honest: It's going to be difficult to swallow.

Chances are, you will be shocked by my advice. You may feel I'm being politically incorrect. A chauvinist. A thoroughly unmodern man. But I challenge you to read this book with an open mind and open heart and let the scripture-based advice reveal God's plan for you and all men. I promise you will feel renewed and invigorated by the journey you are about to take.

According to God's word, man was created and placed on this earth to be a leader, a lover, a servant, a protector, a teacher, a provider, a procreator. Those aren't my words; those words come from God and have been instructing men for centuries. If you don't believe anything else you read here, believe this one thing: God doesn't make mistakes.

While the world wrestles with gender identity, fatherless homes, drug addiction, online pornography, escalating suicide rates, crowded prisons, cancel culture, loss of civility, and gun violence in classrooms, it can be difficult to see God in our midst. I assure you he has not abandoned us, but rather he has empowered us. Imagine how men could change our broken world if we became the leaders God created us to be.

It's not easy to be a man in this damned-if-you-do and damned-if-you-don't society. No matter what we say, there's a long line of people eager to pounce on anyone bold enough to promote traditional values or point out what's clearly right or clearly wrong.

Guys, this is our wake-up call. Our grades for Manhood 101 have been posted and we're failing in nearly every area in which our creator has asked us to lead. We've surrendered to a culture that doesn't like the way their ancestors got things done. We've given up. We've retreated. And now, the world is falling apart and it's mostly because of our passivity.

Fortunately, the source of courage and confidence we require to take a stand can be found in God's word. Our creator offers sage advice and time-tested guidance for being a good father, husband and provider. God shines a bright light on what we must do to be effective lovers, leaders and protectors.

If you want to be a part of the solution to the world's troubles, you must hear God's word and then submit. This is not the time to submit to your wives, Hollywood actors, politicians, or the loudest voices on social media. This is the time to submit to the one and only God and to do what he's always asked men to do.

It's time to call men out. It's time to call men up. As offensive as this may sound to others, it's time to Man Up. It's time to hold each other accountable for our actions. It's time to hold ourselves accountable for our inaction. It's time to speak truth into each other's lives before it's too late. Yes, we risk putting others on the defensive or hurting their feelings. There's an excellent chance we will be canceled by people who otherwise publicly proclaim their tolerance.

It will all be worth it. As men, we've heard this mantra for the better part of our lives: No pain, no gain. We need to reconsider the areas in our life where we've stepped aside because it was easier than taking a stand. To be a man of principle, you may risk relationships that you once thought were important. I challenge you to take those risks, endure the pain, and then relish the rewards that come with being a man of steadfast faith.

We have the power to save our families. We can save our communities and our country. But most importantly, we can play an important part in rebuilding God's kingdom.

The first step to recapturing your power requires having tough conversations with yourself, with those closest to you, and with God. Consider those conversations the medicine that will restore you to the spiritually healthy man God intends you to be.

Fred J. Parry

CHAPTER ONE

The Definition Of A Man

1

What does it mean to be a man in today's world? You could make a case that the definition of a man has changed over time. As society, culture, technology, and human relationships have evolved, so has the definition of what it means to be a man.

For example, in 1577, an English clergyman named William Harrison wrote that he feared manliness was eroding, and he pointed to a specific temptation. A generation before Harrison wrote his missive, the luxury of sleeping on a bed pillow had been reserved for women. Any adult male who dared to lay his weary head on a soft sack of feathers or even straw was considered unmanly. According to Harrison, "a good round log under their heads," should remain the choice of stalwart Elizabethan-era men, but to his dismay, many men were opting for comfort. As someone who enjoys sleeping with my head propped on a pile of pillows, I'm glad that men are no longer judged by that standard.

With all due respect to William Harrison, the proof is not in the pillows. How humankind measures masculinity changes from one generation to the next, but God's definition of manhood is constant. He doesn't expect us to live like those sleep-deprived

Elizabethans or the early Christians who traveled on foot to share the gospel. He doesn't care if we eat from stone bowls or porcelain plates. No matter how the trappings of this earthly kingdom advance and shift, God walks comfortably in our midst and expects us to stand firm as leaders at home and in the world. Yet, we have slowly surrendered the power God gave us.

Before the industrial revolution, most American men were ranchers and farmers. In an agrarian economy, their roles were straightforward. They worked long days and were largely self-sufficient. Their families depended on the crops they grew, the livestock they raised and the game they harvested. Farmers brought up their children to work on the farm, which helped increase productivity and yield. Because members of the household lived and worked together, these men spent a lot more time with their children than we do today.

When the industrial revolution began around the turn of the 19th century, we witnessed a transition from an agrarian economy, where men labored with their hands, to a more dependable manufacturing economy that relied on machinery to do the heavy lifting. The industrial revolution introduced production methods that relied largely on water and steam-powered machinery to increase productivity and efficiency. The work was often less strenuous and was unaffected by weather and other uncontrollable factors that disrupted farming.

The manufacturing sector boomed, incomes grew, and the U.S. population was on the rise. The industrial revolution ushered in cultural changes that altered family structures. The standard of living increased dramatically and that put a different kind of pressure on men to provide more than the basics of food and shelter for their families. Men began to leave the farm to pursue these new opportunities and, as a result, began spending less time with their families.

Steam-powered engines expanded the horizon and narrowed the distances that once seemed unimaginably far. It was an era filled with new opportunities, but it came with a high cost as the relationship between a man and his family changed in a profound way. There was a converse relationship between progress and the once-traditional family structures where men once anchored the households.

In the 1950s, following World War II, the United States saw more dramatic changes that affected family structures and the role of men. During the 20 years following the war, the United States experienced an explosion in the birth rate. The introduction of the Servicemen's Readjustment Act of 1944, also known as the G.I. Bill, created widespread cultural changes by providing economic incentives for war veterans to go to college, buy homes and start businesses. Many men began using their minds instead of their brawn to create economic prosperity for their growing families. As men became savvy at business, they focused on building wealth and working smarter rather than harder.

Over the course of a few decades, masculinity developed. Men went from being measured by their physical effort to being judged by their prowess at intellectual tasks. The dusk-to-dawn work ethic was now part of the past. The definition of what it meant to be a man was also changing.

In the 1960s and '70s, a cultural revolution began to shape man's role in the family. Increases in the cost of living and in the consumption of products and services drove a higher standard of living. The quest for second cars, more bedrooms, and Disneyland vacations meant that many women gave up their singular role as homemakers to join the workforce and supplement their husband's income. With Mom going to work, children did not get the attention they once had, and Dad took on a share of domestic responsibilities once handled exclusively by his wife.

Some sociologists refer to this era as the beginning of the "sissification," where a man's role in the family unit and in society was simultaneously feminized and diminished. Unfortunately, this was a welcome change for some men who felt burdened by the responsibility of providing for their families.

Between the years 2000 and 2012, China's entry into the World Trade Organization triggered the loss of 2 million American jobs. This era, commonly referred to as the China Trade Shock, forced a record number of men into unemployment and into non-manufacturing jobs, which further softened the masculine perception of work while wiping out retirement accounts and men's ability to provide for their families.

As we fast forward to 2025, it's easy to see that modern men look distinctly different from men a few decades ago. We are surrounded by men who seek acceptance by apologizing for the fact that they are men. These same men stand critical of the masculine spirit and believe that all living men should be held accountable for the sins of previous generations. Painting an entire gender with a broad brush and then assigning the sins of the few to the multitude is not only unfair but cowardly.

Earlier this year, the Boy Scouts of America succumbed to public pressure and neutered the name of its 115-year-old organization, changing it to Scouting America. As someone who has been a proud Eagle Scout for more than 45 years, I am ashamed that the institution which played such an influential role in making me a better man is now governed by men who did not have the character or fortitude to stand up to the bullying of angry women and feminized men who wish to further minimize the value that young men contribute to this society. Ironically, no one seems to question the appropriateness of an organization called Girl Scouts of America, which has been in existence for 113 years.

Male passivists and advocates for the feminist movement began to diminish the value of a man's role using messaging along the lines of, "A woman needs a man like a fish needs a bicycle." The tolerance for this demeaning characterization of men grew in popularity as an increasing number of men failed their families and societal obligations. As the percentage of male breadwinners began to diminish, so too did their influence on household matters, including the raising and disciplining of children.

There's plenty that is wrong with today's generation of men, but the decay of the masculine spirit and our relationship with the opposite sex seem to be at the root of why so many men fail miserably at being men. While it's important to respect and honor women, it's also important to set boundaries with the women we love and those with whom we work. Women have an abundance of positive characteristics and attributes. As a man, you should feel compelled to advocate for women. However, there are differences between men and women that should not be ignored. Beyond the physical characteristics, dozens of high-quality university studies have shown significant differences in the brains of men and women. Simply put, men and women perceive and process things in different ways.

In many respects, we deserve exactly what has happened to us as men. We have failed to live up to the responsibilities God instilled in us. Many of us hide behind our careers and put up a facade of busyness to keep others at a safe distance. We're too busy to deal with the kids. Were too busy to lead our families. We lack the confidence to deal with the complicated messes in our lives. We'd like to be in charge, but we'd rather not be responsible for all that comes with it.

Our preference is to hide behind our jobs and retreat into isolation where we don't have to contend with this chaos and overwhelming responsibility. The modern man gets lost in video games, pornography, excessive screen time, and the stacks of work he brings home from the office. He is fearful that being mentally present at home might initiate a moment of intimacy with his wife or a connection point with his kids that he's not emotionally prepared to handle.

The bottom line is that the modern man lacks a sense of self-identity or mission for his life. When an emotionally distant man decides to connect with someone, he is likely to pursue something akin to a tribal relationship, where misery loves company. He'll resist the temptation to connect with men who are emotionally healthy for fear of shining a brighter light on his own insecurity, fear or sense of jealousy. He'd rather find a brotherhood with men who are also insecure and numb to their feelings. The best places to find those guys are at bars, golf courses, or recreational sports leagues where there's no danger of making meaningful connections.

Like the obvious perils of our woundedness, which include broken marriages, damaged relationships, and being emotionally absent fathers, the failures of modern men are deeply destructive on a personal level. We all know men who are dealing with anxiety or depression. We also know men who resort to domestic violence and drug abuse when they lose a grip on their emotions and interpersonal relationships. Today, men are four times more likely than women to die by suicide. Males make up 93 percent of the jail and prison population in the United States. Boys are far more likely than girls to drop out of high school. Almost 99 percent of sexual abuse perpetrators are male. Our inability to keep our emotional affairs in check and deal with our woundedness also affects our longevity; women tend to outlive men by an average of five years.

The news is really disturbing for men whose work once defined their sense of purpose. The median wage for men has fallen in each of the last 20 years. Men make up only 40 percent of the enrollment at universities and colleges. To make matters worse, men are leaving the workforce at an alarming rate. Six decades ago, 97 percent of men between the ages of 25 and 54 were gainfully employed. Today, a whopping 18 percent of men in the same age group are neither working nor seeking employment. Of these unemployed men, nearly half are taking pain medications daily. Experts are on record claiming that the increased use of prescription opioids and technological advances in video game production are driving factors contributing to the growing number of men who are staying home.

Perhaps the most innocent victims of this identity crisis are our sons. They've grown up bombarded with terms like "toxic masculinity," and they've been punished simply for behaving like energetic, rambunctious boys. Boys are disciplined at school for not acting like girls. Boys are twice as likely to be suspended and twice as likely to be medicated for masculine behavior. At the recommendation of teachers, school counselors, and psychiatrists, boys are being pumped full of prescription drugs for attention deficit disorders. The message to our sons is clear: Stop acting like boys! A reasonable child might conclude that, perhaps, it's not good to be a boy. In an era when gender dysphoria, transgenderism, and sex changes for eight-year-olds are prevalent enough to become political fodder, one has to wonder if the negative messages being directed at our sons might play a role in this disturbing trend.

If we're ever going to reverse this decline in the masculine spirit, we're going to have to speak louder than the men who are ashamed to be men. We're going to have to step forward and reclaim lost ground. We've got to come out of isolation and out from behind our work to take back our families. It's one thing to say that you're a man, but it's an altogether different thing to live like a man.

Living like a man means taking responsibility for our own messes and the messes made by other people. Living like a man has nothing to do with how many pounds you can bench press or how much money you make. It doesn't require Adonis-like looks or even a tattoo.

Being a man ain't easy, but being a good man is even tougher.

The Characteristics Of A Good Man

Every now and then, you'll hear one man instruct another to "Man up," or "Act like a real man!" These are thinly veiled calls to ramp up the testosterone and be more aggressive and assertive. Unfortunately, we rarely challenge someone to be a "good man." There's a stark difference between being a "real man" and being a "good man." We should all strive to be good men, but what does it mean to be a good man in this modern era? The good news is that the definition hasn't changed for centuries.

Here are a few of the characteristics that define a good man:

1. A good man is unafraid to show compassion and empathy toward others.
2. A good man is honest and knows that the truth, no matter how difficult, wins the day.
3. A good man protects, provides for, and presides over his family.
4. A good man exudes humility and puts the needs of others before his own.
5. A good man practices temperance in all things and lives by moderation and self-restraint.
6. A good man is a man of his word and honors the promises he makes, both big and small.
7. A good man does not have to be reminded of his obligations to his family, friends, and others.

8. A good man is determined, resilient, and passionate in all endeavors.
9. A good man lives in accordance with a prescribed set of core values and a mission for his life.
10. A good man is a loving parent and readily provides for the physical, emotional and spiritual needs of his family.
11. A good man is altruistic in all areas of his life and seeks no recognition for his generosity.
12. A good man is courageous and remains calm during life's storms.

The Problem With Men Today

Boys run away from difficult situations. Men run toward them.

Passivity is to blame for the failings of modern-day men. We've allowed the mass media, men who are ashamed to be men, and a movement of angry, bitter women to push us into a corner where we have been forced to accept the blame for a generation of lost men who have made horrifically bad decisions. The increase in fatherless homes and the steady retreat of soft men have emboldened a crusade to remove men from the centers of influence they once occupied. They've got us where they want us, but there's still a chance to reverse course and rise to the standard God established for men with the creation of Adam.

Men are facing a crisis of epidemic proportions. We've been pushed to the point where the purpose of our existence is always in question, and we're fighting the uphill battle of trying to get our lives back in order while nursing our self-inflicted wounds. It's a difficult time to be a man and that's left a lot of guys asking themselves the question, "What's wrong with me?" In truth, there's a lot wrong with us. Some of our problems are deeply psychological, while others could be fixed with a swift kick in the pants. Let's look at why so many men are struggling.

THE PURSUIT OF ELUSIVE JOY

If you feel like you're living in a state of constant dissatisfaction, you're not alone. Some sociologists suggest we've inadvertently programmed ourselves into believing that both our past and future are better than our present lives. It's easy to be optimistic about the future; everyone's allowed to dream. But it's almost a certainty that our level of contentment 20 years from now is going to be on par with how we feel today.

When you think about it, if we were completely content with our lives, wouldn't we lose our drive to push for a better future? We're stuck in a state of self-deception where we've convinced ourselves that we must keep working harder for a better tomorrow.

In addition to our rosy vision of the future, we tend to romanticize the past. We choose to remember pleasant experiences from our past and block memories of the not-so-good times. We fondly remember our childhood, our high school days, and who could ever forget the great times we had on campus when we didn't have a care in the world? Really? We've somehow erased the stress of studying, the heartaches of young romance, and our frustration with roommates, professors and disgusting cafeteria food. If we're honest, we had just as many troubles in the old days as we do today. Troubles never go away, and we'll contend with our fair share during our highly anticipated golden years. That's life!

We believe that getting our affairs in order for the future requires keeping our noses to the grindstone so one day we can live comfortably. When we finally arrive in the future, we'll find a new set of problems waiting. Again, that's life!

You've heard the Latin phrase carpe diem, which literally translates to "pluck the day" or the more widely used translation, "seize the day." It's a worthwhile reminder to live every day as if it's our last. Live for the moment. Enjoy life today. Stop worrying about tomorrow and forget about the past. Smell the roses. Take a big bite out of the apple. You've heard all of these phrases before, but have you actually given that advice a try?

> *"Therefore do not worry about tomorrow, for tomorrow will worry about itself. Each day has enough trouble of its own."*
> MATTHEW 6:34 NIV

You could spend the rest of your life looking for the joy that you could have today if only you'd take your foot off the gas and enjoy the moment. They say that happiness is an occasional visitor who pops in from time to time and never overstays her welcome. If you were happy and joyful all the time, you'd probably tire of that emotion and lose your will to seek a better future. Take a deep breath and savor the moments of joy when they come.

LOST HOPE

Hope gives us the resilience to push forward and find reasons for living. We often lose hope when we lose an important connection. This loss could be the death of a loved one, a divorce, or a major unexpected change. When this connection is taken from us, we tend to lose hope.

There are times when exhaustion or burnout saps us of hope. When we can't manage our responsibilities or fail to achieve important goals, hope seems fleeting. We become discouraged by our circumstances and the idea of digging ourselves out of the hole feels overwhelming.

We can restore hope by focusing on small, incremental things we can control that will move our lives in a positive direction. We should set realistic, attainable goals for ourselves, and when we achieve these small tasks, our confidence will grow. We can then gain courage to pursue the next goal and the next … each step brings us closer to solid ground.

Hope can find its footing through new connections and the interpersonal relationships we so desperately need. Join a club. Go to church. Sign up for a class. Never underestimate the power of human connection. It will give you hope for greater things.

LONELINESS

We're beginning to understand the advantages of building and staying connected with other human beings. The long months of the COVID-19 pandemic were a setback in so many ways. In addition to the physical illness, the pandemic triggered psychological maladies by forcing people into isolation. Some would go for days, even weeks without any form of human interaction.

The United States Surgeon General released a report in 2023 announcing an epidemic of loneliness in our country. The condition is said to have led to increases in cardiovascular disease, diabetes, high blood pressure and other risk factors that can lead to early death. One study of loneliness showed that it can have the same health impact as smoking 15 cigarettes a day. The risk factors are the same for those who may appear to be in the middle of a crowd but still feel isolated. They lack companionship or true friends who will be there for them. The stress associated with loneliness can take an astonishing toll on your long-term health.

Men tend to gravitate toward isolation, often by choice. They will retreat to a place where they can't be held accountable or responsible, and the adverse impact on their health is a real concern. We are called to pull other men from isolation and, hopefully, someone will do the same for us if we need it.

> *"My brothers and sisters, if one of you should wander from the truth and someone should bring that person back, remember this: Whoever turns a sinner from the error of their way will save them from death and cover over a multitude of sins."*
> **JAMES 5:19-20 NIV**

EXHAUSTION

Men underestimate the value of rest because they equate it with a lack of productivity. When it comes to embracing the restorative values of rest, men are sabotaged by their own work ethic. Our egos prevent us from admitting that our bodies need a break. Rest, for many of us, is a sign of weakness.

Getting rest is not about getting to bed early or sleeping an extra hour on Saturday morning. More than 75 percent of the energy we need to survive comes from sources of rest other than sleep. Experts believe we need social rest—a time when we can unwind in the company of good friends and family members. They also recommend mental rest that comes from stepping away from our responsibilities, if only for a short time, to unplug and mentally recharge. Finally, men need spiritual rest when they can connect in solitude with their higher power to reflect, set goals and put life in perspective. The physical rest that comes from sleep won't overcome a shortage of these other essential forms of rest. Another important contributor to our overall health is dealing proactively with physical ailments that may affect the way we feel. Undiagnosed medical conditions such as diabetes, thyroid disease, depression and sleep apnea can rob us of energy and a general sense of wellness. It's critical that we pay attention to what our bodies are telling us. Though no one likes to be reminded, exercise and good nutrition can also make an crucial difference.

UNRESOLVED TRAUMA

You rarely hear guys talking about unresolved trauma in their lives. In fact, many men don't realize they may have trauma issues that they haven't appropriately processed. This condition is related to an intensely disturbing event or incident earlier in their lives that overwhelmed the brain's capacity for tolerance.

Unresolved trauma may be connected to a serious car accident, combat experience, illness or sexual abuse that overloaded the circuits of your brain. The emotional damage associated with an incident prevents you from processing the experience in a manner consistent with the way you've handled other events in your life. The shock, confusion and terror may have caused you to block it from your memory or stow it deep inside your brain.

The suppression of memories can instill in men a deep desire to maintain control at all times. They may distrust others or refuse to let their guard down. Repressed memories can drive a man's desire to be in control at all times and at any cost.

Common symptoms of unresolved trauma include anger issues, poor sleep, and low self-esteem. If you're familiar with Post Traumatic Stress Disorder (PTSD), you might know that this mental health condition is a form of unresolved trauma where those afflicted will experience flashbacks, nightmares and extreme anxiety. The only effective way to treat this type of trauma is with the help of a psychiatric professional.
If you suspect that some of your untoward behaviors may be connected to undetected trauma from earlier in your life, seek out a counseling professional trained to help you safely explore this issue.

Life is complicated. When we as men fail to set aside our pride and consider the factors that affect our health, we do a tremendous disservice to ourselves. When we bravely address our loneliness, poor health habits, hopelessness, and the possibility of unresolved trauma, we can progress toward becoming the best version of ourselves.

Confronting Our Demons

MIND THE GAP

The term "mind the gap" was coined in the 1960s by the London Underground transit system. The intention was to warn passengers of the gap between the train car and the station platform. It was a courtesy and a reminder to be aware of potential danger. This warning is still used today. Wouldn't it be nice if we had warning signs to protect us all along life's journey? As men, we could use frequent reminders to watch our steps.

Navigating life is treacherous because so much of what we experience is not as it initially seems. We can take nothing at face value. There's always some emotion or unprocessed trauma lurking in the shadows, ready to spring from its hiding place to attack.

Our emotional backstory is revealed when we feel threatened, powerless or invalidated. Our emotions feed into our fight-or-flight instincts. Hormones mobilize our body's resources as we process whether we're going to dig in and deal with a problem or retreat to safety. Our reactions can be unpredictable, and there's no telling how much collateral damage will be left after the bedlam.

At the core of this unseemly behavior are our insecurities, low self-esteem, fears, frustrations and a lack of healthy human relationships in our lives. We haven't been taught the proper coping strategies for properly processing these emotions.

As our traditionally masculine roles have been redefined by a culture war, men have allowed themselves to be put at a disadvantage. Rather than claim our honest emotions and rightful leadership roles, we've retreated to dark corners and we've let our worst impulses take over.

It's time to confront the demons that keep us from becoming the best version of ourselves. Information is power, and to make progress, we must identify where we're vulnerable so that we can rise again to lead our families and communities and begin rebuilding God's kingdom.

CONTROLLING OTHERS

In most cases, our desperation to maintain absolute control over our lives can be traced to anxiety born out of fear, low self-esteem and insecurity. The seeds for these negative attributes are often planted through cruel comments or abusive treatment by authority figures like parents, teachers, coaches and scouting leaders, and they grow unchecked in impressionable minds. Men who try to exert control in every situation may be dealing with insecurities that causes them to fear things will go wrong if they're not in charge.

Are you a man who believes the world would be better if those around you did things the way you want them done? You may recognize controlling behavior when you criticize something as insignificant as how a bed is made or how another person drives a car.

Most often, a man's need to exert control is triggered by a lack of trust in those with whom he is dealing. You've heard the tired phrase, "If I want something done right, I'm going to have to do it myself." When you hear those words coming from someone else, or out of your own mouth, you can generally assume there's a control issue at play.

Not all attempts to exert control are linked to a man's fears or insecurity. In some cases, control is used to assert dominance over another person. In this case, it enters the realm of abuse and may need to be dealt with by law enforcement or by a trained counseling professional.

If you're someone with control issues, changing your behavior begins with a process of self-reflection and self-awareness. When you feel yourself begin to power up or get angry, search your soul to determine what triggered this reaction. Then, dig a little deeper. Our initial inclination is very rarely the core issue.

ANGER

There can be a strong correlation between our need for control and the anger we carry. Much of how we react is often tied on our interpretation of an event or series of events. You've probably seen someone react to a seemingly minor incident with an angry outburst and thought to yourself, "Wow! That was an overreaction." You jumped to that conclusion without having a full understanding of his lived experiences or the emotional context of his current circumstances. Your instincts are likely correct.

Anger comes charging in when we feel threatened, powerless, invalidated or disrespected. It may be impossible for us to understand the gamut of emotions behind an outburst by someone else or even ourselves. To complicate matters, we all process and express anger differently, depending on the coping skills we learned early in life. Some of us were taught to express our disappointment verbally, which gives others a chance to understand the emotions behind our anger. Unfortunately, many men were taught to suppress their anger and deal with the ramifications internally without sharing their feelings with anyone, including loved ones.

Others have mastered passive-aggressive behavior, where there is inconsistency between their words and actions. They will smile at you, but behind your back, they are shooting daggers at you. They resent your power to make them feel unworthy, even when you have no such intention. They fear rejection and so they say one thing but do another. Today's workplaces are filled with passive-aggressive people who struggle to appropriately process their insecurity.

Perhaps the most damaging type of anger is tied to betrayal. When a confidence or trust has been violated, we feel invalidated. Our spirit is crushed. The whole foundation of our belief systems has been wiped out by another person's duplicity. Reconciliation is unlikely because trust has been destroyed. Anger borne out of betrayal leads men to a very lonely place.

Whether expressed through words or actions, anger is a choice we make. God gives you the freedom to choose your response in every situation. Nothing productive comes from anger, so your best option is to choose not to be angry. Mark Twain once said that anger is an acid that can do more harm to the vessel in which it is stored than to anything on which it is poured. That timeless piece of good advice will serve you well.

ADDICTION

Alcohol and drug addiction can take root when men don't properly contend with unprocessed emotions. Because many men believe that a release of emotions equates with weakness, they look for other ways to numb their pain.

Alcoholism and substance abuse are attributed to a blend of genetic risk factors and a long list of environmental triggers. Research has shown that men tend to be more vulnerable to substance abuse than women, and men have more tolerant and permissive attitudes toward alcohol and drug use. Perhaps you've heard the term, "If it feels good, do it!" This laissez-faire attitude harms us and contributes to much larger problems.

One factor driving men to indulge in drugs and alcohol is a lack of healthy relationships. Unlike women, we rarely have relationships that allow us to confide in one another about our troubles and fears. We are more likely to find comfort in a bottle of alcohol enjoyed with buddies who are unwilling to engage each other about the things that drive us to drink. It's a cycle that often spirals out of control. Women, on the other hand, discuss their emotions, fears and frustrations with their girlfriends. Men typically find that level of vulnerability to be extraordinarily uncomfortable.

Boys begin jockeying for position on the masculinity scale at an early age. By the time they are teenagers, they are eager to prove they can roll with the big boys. They try to impress their peers with the volume and speed at which they consume alcohol. Unfortunately, the more men drink, the more their inhibitions retreat, freeing them up to talk crap. Testosterone takes over from there. Men do stupid things when they drink and that earns them membership into a brotherhood with exceedingly low standards.

When we eventually discover we can mask our pain with drugs and alcohol, we use and abuse them more frequently. Soon, we're shackled with a bad habit. What initially felt like a harmless escape becomes a lifestyle choice that spins out of control. For those who are genetically prone to addiction, it's a story that rarely has a happy ending.

ISOLATION

The truth about men is that we'd rather compete than connect.

Some might say that's how we're wired, but that's really just a lame excuse for unhealthy behavior. Almost every aspect of our lives depends on social interaction. Our most basic forms of survival depend on relationships with other humans, so it's odd that most men would simply prefer not to interact at any level.

This propensity is not written into the male DNA; it's learned behavior. Our culture discourages young men and boys from showing emotion. There's only one exception: boys are taught that it's appropriate to express anger. You can imagine how problematic that becomes when those boys grow up and interact with other humans—spouses, co-workers, or misbehaving children.

In contrast, women possess a deeper appreciation for the values of warmth, compassion and empathy. Women are often better at social interaction, and some would say, they crave it.

Men require a clearly defined purpose behind social interaction. We'll engage in social activity if it involves eating food or consuming alcohol. For men, social interaction must be efficient and purpose-driven. Before the pandemic, men found most of their interactions with other men came through their jobs, sports, or through hobbies such as hunting and fishing. Amid the COVID-19 lockdowns and social distancing policies, those connections vanished and, sadly, many of those activities did not resume post-pandemic. You rarely find men gathering simply for the sake of gathering. It's not until much later in life that men start meeting friends at a coffee shop for the sole purpose of social interaction ... and a good cinnamon glazed donut!

If you want to bring men together for social engagement, you'd better have a purpose in mind. Men want to build something or tear something apart. Men need a project where they can demonstrate their masculinity while in the presence of other men. That's why projects like Habitat for Humanity or mission trips to build schools in third-world countries are appealing to men.

Unfortunately, men seem predisposed to exist in isolation. It's a safe place. There's nobody there to ask questions or compete with you. But men often engage in self-destructive behavior when they're in isolation. It's during these times when they are most likely to gravitate toward alcohol, drugs and pornography. Self-pity flourishes in isolation. It is fertile ground for Satan's work. The evil one wants nothing more than to pull us away from others so he can have our full attention. Isolation breeds desperation and that's, unfortunately, where thoughts of harming ourselves can develop.

When someone notices an isolated man and tries to help, the man's natural response is almost always, "I'm good!" The average disconnected person will take his response at face value and move on to other things. A caring person will call his bluff and work to pull him back into the light. As Christian men, we must be intentional in our efforts and challenge the behaviors of men who have isolated themselves. This can feel risky. We must have the courage to engage the men we see slipping away. It's possible, even likely, that they will view accepting our help as a sign of weakness. Help anyway.

Working to pull another man out of isolation is a double-edged sword. The man you're trying to help will believe that letting you inside his turbulent world requires a vulnerability and transparency that feels dangerous to him. If you are rejected by this man while trying to help him, you will feel the painful sting of rejection. But without risk, there is no reward. Forge ahead with the confidence of knowing that God rewards our risks when we act in love and compassion on behalf of another person who needs our help.

TEMPTATION

The smallest temptations can lead to the biggest sins.

No matter how disciplined you may be, you'll never be exempt from the work of the evil one, who is constantly plotting to drive a wedge between you and God. Fortunately, God has equipped us with ways to protect ourselves from temptation, and he helps us stand firm in the face of the evil that tries to lure us into darkness.

> *"No temptation has overtaken you except what is common to mankind. And God is faithful; he will not let you be tempted beyond what you can bear. But when you are tempted, he will also provide a way out so that you can endure it ...."*
> **1 CORINTHIANS 10:13 NIV**

The devil's no fool. He's strategic in his tactics because he knows exactly where we are weakest. If a man struggles with sexual curiosity, Satan is going to set traps in that area of his life. If a man is envious and covets something that belongs to another person, the devil is going to expose that weakness at the most inopportune time. The temptations we face will take root in the soil made fertile by our lack of faith and conviction. The devil convinces us that we're not strong enough to resist temptation. When we feel most vulnerable, we must remember to lean into our faith and take up the shield God has given us to defend ourselves from temptation. The bottom line is that we need

God during these trying times. No matter how resolute we may seem, the devil can wear us down. He makes us believe we are defenseless and then uses temptation to ruin our lives. As men, we get caught in a pattern of sin. We are seduced by the promise of pleasure, and, like Samson, we engage in destructive behavior for the sake of temporary sinful gratification.

To gain victory over temptation, we must first acknowledge our weaknesses and then build our defenses. We must prepare our hearts and minds for the most important battle we will ever fight. We must remember God's promises and stand convicted to honor him by protecting our hearts from the sinfulness that lurks. When the battle begins in earnest, we can always take refuge in our Holy Father.

> *"Every word of God is flawless; he is a shield to those who take refuge in him."* PROVERBS 30:5 NIV

LACK OF SELF-AWARENESS

Sometimes we don't see ourselves the same way others see us. Engaging in intentional self-reflection and trying to understand the motivations behind our actions as well as the thoughts and emotions that drive these actions is a critical step toward living a more fulfilled life.

Gaining understanding about why we do and say certain things can help us to grow personally, enhance our relationships, improve our decision-making, and face things we have been avoiding.

While increasing your self-awareness is decidedly beneficial, it can be a painful and arduous process. Self-reflection begins with a level of honesty that is awkward and uncomfortable. It can make us defensive. If you're serious about digging deeper into your personality and finding out what's behind that outburst of anger or bout of depression, you must undertake some serious self-contemplation.

To succeed in becoming more self-aware, mentally replay the episodes of your life when your behavior surprised you or seemed incongruent with the emotions you were feeling. This work requires serious focus. Quiet the world around you and meditate on the timeline of events that have fueled certain emotions.

PRIDE

If there's one sin voted most likely to lead men down a path to destruction, it's pride. Pride is the byproduct when you indulge in a deep level of satisfaction about your personal achievements. It's pride that gives men an inflated opinion of their talent, ability and the value they bring to relationships.

The overconfidence that comes with pride can delude us about what we actually contribute to society. There's a reason that pride is one of the seven deadly sins. When we are prideful, we discount the contributions of others and see ourselves as more important than others. Like so many of our destructive behaviors, pride is born out of low self-esteem and an unwillingness to be vulnerable and authentic in the presence of others.

> *"For by the grace given me I say to every one of you: Do not think of yourself more highly than you ought, but rather think of yourself with sober judgment, in accordance with the faith God has distributed to each of you."* ROMANS 12:3 NIV

Pride is often the glitzy mask we wear to camoflage larger problems. A person who is prideful may be impeccably dressed and have a beautiful wife on his arm. He may drive an expensive sports car and live in the best neighborhood. A prideful man finds it important to convey a message that he has his life under control. It's all a façade. A man's laser-like focus on his own needs makes it impossible for him to have authentic relationships with others. A man consumed by pride lacks compassion for others and this makes him unwilling to put others before himself. In Philippians 2:3-4, we read, "Do nothing out of selfish ambition or vain conceit. Rather, in humility value others above yourselves, not looking to your own interests but each of you to the interests of the others."

COMPARISON

Theodore Roosevelt said, "Comparison is the thief of joy." Roosevelt understood that comparing your life with someone else's was fruitless because you lack a complete picture of that person's life. On the other hand, you are intensely familiar with the messiness of your own life.

As competitive creatures, men often obsess over how we stack up against other men. We all know someone who lives in a nicer house, drives a faster car and, thanks to superior genetics, has a better physique. Our identity and self-worth get tangled up with how we compare to others.

It doesn't help that our friends and acquaintances share only the best aspects of their lives on social media. We've all seen the family photos with the impeccably coiffed kids wearing identical outfits on the beach in Hawaii. We've seen the photos of a buddy pulling the perfectly cooked slab of ribs off the grill, which he has strategically placed on the driveway next to his new Corvette. Don't forget the photos of your cousin's new pool and cabana house at their vacation home in Vail.

Although we understand, intellectually, that our Facebook friends are putting their best face on social media, it still triggers feelings of inadequacy. Social media creates unrealistic standards. Even when that blissful family on the Hawaiian beach files for bankruptcy and their marriage dissolves in divorce, we fail to comprehend that the happy-looking couple wasn't happy at all.

Not only do comparison and envy steal our joy, they erode our self-esteem and disconnect us from relationships that really matter. The key is to be yourself and live your own dreams. Let other people see the real you. Allow them to discover your uniqueness and enjoy the companionship you provide.

One of the best ways to reject comparison is to practice gratitude. Take a moment to reflect on the many blessings you have in your life. Be thankful for the abundance of gifts that God has given you. Gratitude will give you an appropriate context for the life you already have.

REJECTION

We've all been rejected at some point. You might have met rejection on the playground when you were the last one picked to play dodgeball. Perhaps you encountered rejection when the elite, competitive, middle-school sports league passed over your child. As we mature, the rejection we face becomes more personal and hurtful. Maybe you didn't get an expected work promotion, or your girlfriend breaks things off. The sting of rejection is real, and it can change the way men perceive ourselves and those around us.

Rejection can leave you feeling depressed, left out, and invisible to others. You're confronted with the reality that life isn't always fair. Rejection can also make you feel resentful.

If you face rejection, avoid ruminating over the reasons. Don't ask, "What's wrong with me?" Instead, channel your energies into careful self-reflection and focus on the opportunities you have for improvement. Could you make yourself more professionally or physically attractive if you put in some effort? Now is the time to focus on the strengths and positive attributes that make you a likable or successful person. Ask yourself, "What can I learn from this experience? How can I move forward?"

Rejection can motivate you to consider lifestyle changes that improve your health and outlook on life. How are your sleep patterns, dietary choices and exercise habits contributing to your well-being? Making positive changes in any of these areas will improve your overall performance. When you feel better about yourself, others will feel better about you.

There are positive things that can come from rejection. Some people take it as a challenge and begin working to prove wrong the person who rejected them. Rejection can make us more resilient, inspiring us to work harder to achieve all we hope for.

LACK OF SELF-CONTROL

> *"Like a city whose walls are broken through is a person who lacks self-control."* PROVERBS 25:28 NIV

At the heart of most of man's problems is his lack of self-control. As the verse above references, we are subject to great danger when we fail to exercise self-control. We are defenseless against things like lust, greed, envy, wickedness, and all the temptations that bring us temporary pleasure. Without some sense of power over these things, we'll find ourselves either incarcerated or living a lonely and isolated life.

The behaviors that we think are harmless may be filled with danger. Maybe you're a road-rager who lays on the horn when someone drives the speed limit in the passing lane. You might be engrossed by whatever's happening on your smartphone and missing quality time with your family. Perhaps you're triggered by a scantily clad woman in a television commercial and retreat to the nearest bathroom to surf pornography. Maybe you're guilty of all these things, and if you are, you're not alone.

Standing strong and resistant to life's temptations changes men's lives for the better. Some of us struggle to control our words, and others are slaves to their gluttonous appetites. It can be a battle to keep anger and frustration in check. We may know all the strategies necessary to avoid the triggers, but sooner or later, we will surrender to our weaknesses and give in to sin.

Conquering our temptations takes extraordinary effort. You may walk three feet in the right direction, then slide back four. You can overcome any challenge, but you must want to succeed. Build your wall of resistance slowly, one brick at a time. To make these changes permanent, surrender to God and ask him to be strong on your behalf when you are weak.

Winning at self-control requires hard work, humility, self-awareness and a deep and abiding faith in God. You've got this!

> *"Nothing in the world is worth having or worth doing unless it means effort, pain, difficulty … I have never in my life envied a human being who led an easy life. I have envied a great many people who led difficult lives and led them well."*
> —THEODORE ROOSEVELT

THE EVOLUTION OF MAN

It used to be easier to be a man. Once you mastered the art of hunting, gathering and lovemaking, you pretty much had life figured out. As man evolved and began to stand upright and wear shoes, life got more complicated but, for the most part, the role of provider and protector remained a straightforward responsibility with few distractions.

Today, men are so much more than hunters and gatherers. In addition to providing, protecting, and competently repairing small engines, men are expected to be emotionally engaged, sensitive, smart and self-aware. That's a lot of pressure and if we weren't so filled with pride, we might be able to admit that we're feeling a little overwhelmed.

When the stress associated with the length of our "to-do" lists finally catches up with us, it takes a toll on our physical state and affects our cardiovascular, digestive and mental wellness. Because we're so good at masking our discomfort, the outside world doesn't have a clue that we're in trouble until we lash out in anger or withdraw into isolation.

When someone is brave enough to ask, "What's wrong?" we might mumble a vague answer about our frustration with a co-worker. Very rarely is that the honest answer, but admitting anything else is akin to confessing weakness. It's not considered masculine to acknowledge our struggle with the normal stuff life throws at us. Sharing our worries with others risks the forfeiture of our "Man Card."

CHAPTER TWO

Reversing The Tide

It's Time To Step Up and Lead

Too many boys are being raised almost exclusively by women in fatherless homes. These boys will get the love and compassion they need from their mothers, but they're not going to be exposed to things that instill a masculine spirit in them. These boys will also learn a great deal from their mothers, but they won't witness the mental toughness and fortitude that a father demonstrates. Granted, there are plenty of bad habits they can learn from an ineffective, detached and absent father, but a good father can make an enormous difference in the way a boy develops into a man. With a father who is fully present, a boy can more easily understand the responsibilities that come with being a man who protects, provides for and presides over his family.

To make up for the shortcomings of men who abandoned their responsibilities to their children, the rest of us must step up to fill in the gaps. There are opportunities to mentor, coach and teach boys the life lessons that will help them become good men. Adding a positive male influence to a boy's life can change families for generations to come.

Embrace Our Differences

It should be obvious that there are considerable differences in the physical and emotional makeup of men and women. If we don't acknowledge these differences, we make the mistake of assuming that women and men are equal in their capabilities to provide certain needs for their children. There are things that only men can contribute to their children's development and the same can be said for women. It's a growing falsehood that children can be raised without the participation of their fathers. That may be true in terms of providing for a child's physical needs, but nothing could be further from the truth when it comes to his or her emotional development. Sons need to witness how a man should treat his family and others. Daughters should witness how a good man treats a woman. Her relationship with her father will have a significant impact on her choice for a husband. Men and women must find ways to work together to raise children. Doing so is our only hope for seeing our children mature into emotionally healthy adults.

Make Your Marriage A Priority

It's a fact that fatherless homes are a common denominator for men who have been incarcerated, experienced drug and alcohol abuse, and abandoned their families. Men who grew up without a positive male influence are even more likely to pass on this curse to the next generation. While divorce rates in the United States have fallen in recent years, so too has the number of couples who are getting married. Among the common reasons for divorce are financial problems, substance abuse, and domestic violence, but "lack of commitment" was listed as the top reason for divorce in the United States.

There was a time when marriage vows were sacred, built stronger by relationships that were not disposable. The biggest casualty of divorce is what it does to the family structure and, specifically, the impact it has on children. Judges seem predisposed to give custody to mothers because so many fathers have failed in their obligations to their children. The emotional and psychological damage done to youngsters because of divorcing parents is devastating. Children of divorced parents often suffer academically, lose interest in social activity, experience heightened feelings of guilt and anger, and are more prone to sickness. The collateral damage on children is reason enough to stay in your marriage, no matter how challenging it may be.

Divorce should be your last result. Few couples have perfect marriages. Building a strong marriage takes a tremendous amount of work over a long period of time. If you're living in a troubled marriage, don't try to fix it yourself. See a marriage counselor or seek guidance from another couple with a strong and healthy marriage. You'll discover that even the happiest of couples experience setbacks and disappointments. Work through your pain and frustration together as husband and wife. Don't be ashamed to ask for help. Given the decay of family structures over the last 50 years, many of us were deprived of good role models for marriage. Staying married is tough, but giving your children a healthy living environment and a model for an enduring marriage is worth the work.

I've always been a believer that if you need a license to drive a car, go fishing or own an exotic pet, you should need a license to become a parent. Unfortunately, nature doesn't work that way. A lot of nice people turn out to be awful parents. Because of their selfishness and lack of preparedness, people with great intentions end up doing more harm than good to their children's emotional development. Men who grew up in fatherless houses as a result of divorce or abandonment don't have a clue that they should stick around and be responsible for the lives they have created. As a result, successive generations of men create one bad situation after another, which inevitably gives the entire gender a bad name.

We can reverse the course of this trend by taking ownership of our actions and living like good men ought to live. If we don't answer this call, we will continue to lose ground and forfeit our right to have a seat at life's table.

Overcoming Temptation

Regardless of where you are on your faith journey, temptations will come your way. God's word tells us we have the power to stand firm against temptation.

> *"No temptation has overtaken you except what is common to mankind. And God is faithful; he will not let you be tempted beyond what you can bear. But when you are tempted, he will also provide a way out so that you can endure it."*
> 1 CORINTHIANS 10:13 NIV

This verse is an assurance that God has given us strength, confidence and ability to overcome temptation.

Here are a couple of tips that can help:

- Limit your access to things that might tempt you. Let out of sight be out of mind and don't be overly confident that you can withstand the temptation. The devil understands our weakest points and uses them to lure us toward evil. Don't fall into his trap.
- There is a distinction between temptation and sin. Don't succumb to sin because you believe that you have already committed it by thinking about it. Just because you're tempted doesn't mean you have to sin.
- Don't disount how your mind and body work with each other. They are more in sync than you might imagine. What affects one likely affects the other, and what one desires can be satisfied by the other.
- Rest is essential for our spirituality. We are more likely to move toward sin when we are tired. We are more vulnerable and lack full control when our energy is low. Rest up so your defenses can be strong and resilient.

"So I find this law at work: Although I want to do good, evil is right there with me. For in my inner being I delight in God's law; but I see another law at work in me, waging war against the law of my mind and making me a prisoner of the law of sin at work within me." ROMANS 7:21–23 NIV

Four Ways To Overcome Temptation:

- Recognize when you are being tempted.
- Before you can fight an enemy, you need to recognize your enemy. You cannot fight an enemy that you do not know or acknowledge. Ask God to grant you a discerning spirit.
- Reduce temptation by shifting your focus to another activity.

- If you've given a particular temptation too much power in your mental sphere, knock it off its pedestal. Reduce the significance of these desires by shifting your attention to something that will reset your focus.

YOUR SPIRITUAL RESPONSE TO TEMPTATION

God is always faithful and will not let you be tempted beyond your ability to handle that temptation. Whatever temptation you encounter, God believes you can handle it. He has faith in you. Use this knowledge to strengthen your confidence and perseverance.

God's word also says he provides a way of escape. He is ready to come to your rescue. You only need to ask for his help. Pray for protection from sin and ask others to pray on your behalf. Extra heads bowed in prayer can make a remarkable difference. Pray fervently and ask God to provide an escape plan.

> *"No temptation has overtaken you except what is common to mankind. And God is faithful; he will not let you be tempted beyond what you can bear. But when you are tempted, he will also provide a way out so that you can endure it."*
> 1 CORINTHIANS 10:13 NIV

Overcoming Adversity

All our trials are God-sent to prompt transformation in our lives (James 1:2-4). We are not made to endure trials for the fun of it. God calls us to endure adversity (Philippians 1:29). Our response determines whether we will benefit from the experience.

In responding to adversity, we must:

- Avoid self-pity. (2 Corinthians 13:5)
- Be slow to anger. (Proverbs 19:11)
- Resist blaming others. (Matthew 7-3:5)
- Avoid self-condemnation. (Ephesians 2:10)
- Resist fear and despair. (Psalm 46:1-3)
- Avoid the temptation to give up. (James 1:12)
- Place our complete faith in Jesus. (Hebrews 13:5-6)
- Surrender to God's will for our lives. (Romans 8:1)
- Take ownership of our faults and accept the responsibility to move forward. (Philippians 4:13)
- Take an eternal perspective. (2 Corinthians 4:18)
- Recognize that it's not the end of the world. God has BIG plans for you. (Romans 16:20)

Resilient Christian men roll up their sleeves and take care of those who are less fortunate. They befriend the isolated and the vulnerable. They recognize those in need and act. God wants us to be resilient so that we can stand between adversity and those being battered by life's storms.

Remember the Navy SEALs' "40% Rule"? When our minds are telling us we're finished, our bodies are only 40% finished! Keep pushing knowing you have another 60% of your strength in reserve.

We are constantly exposed to nonbiblical beliefs through our social contacts, mass media, relationships, co-workers, and whatever series we're watching on Netflix. All of us must stop drinking society's toxic poison and distance ourselves from the things that contaminate our minds. We must resist the temptation to contribute to the toxicity. The words from our mouths reveal the content of our hearts. (Luke 6:45)

PRACTICE SELF CARE

If you do not take care of yourself, it will become increasingly difficult to take care of people around you and the work God has committed into your hands. Stay attuned to your physical, emotional and psychological needs and tend to them with rest, relaxation, decompression, nutrition, meditation and exercise. God promises to meet all our needs, even in the most challenging times. He is always faithful and does not make promises he cannot keep. Instead of turning to unhealthy vices to survive, lean on the word of God to reclaim your hope.

SET BOUNDARIES

The primary purpose of boundaries is to determine which responsibilities are yours and which responsibilities belong to someone else. Boundaries are less about keeping others out and more about setting parameters in your relationships.

We all must make choices, and each choice comes with a set of consequences. Like Newton's third law of physics, "To every action, there is an equal and opposite reaction." The same is true in relationships. Some will be healthy. Some will be toxic and threatening to your personal well-being. Ask God for the discernment you need in managing these relationships. As Christians, we are called to take ownership of our thoughts, feelings and actions. Choose what you want to allow into your space and what should stay outside your boundary.

BOOK RECOMMENDATION

Read *Boundaries: When to Say Yes. How to Say No to Take Control of Your Life* by Henry Cloud and John Townsend.

When We Encounter Toxic Relationships...

- Pray about it. Ask God for wisdom when dealing with this troublesome person.
- Take ownership of the issues that are your responsibility and let go of the ones that aren't.
- Create a set of consequences for the person whose behavior is unacceptable and then follow through.

Remember that boundaries don't have to be permanent walls; they can be temporary fences that are taken down once circumstances improve. The discernment given to you by the Holy Spirit will help you set boundaries and choose the correlating consequences that protect your space and balance the drama in your life.

BE GRATEFUL

Gratitude is the secret to abundance. When we show God that we are grateful and consider ourselves privileged to have what we have, to be loved by him, and to enjoy his abundance, he is inclined to entrust us with even greater blessings.

Tips On Living A Life Of Gratitude:

- Find a way to be content in every moment. (Philippians 4:11)
- Focus on God's constant presence. (Psalm 139:7)
- Connect with the Holy Spirit so that your mind can be renewed and grateful. Even when we are not mindful of what we should be grateful for, the Holy Spirit can remind us. (Romans 12:2)
- Intentionally and proactively look for signs of God's presence in your daily life—in good times and in challenging circumstances.

- Make a list of times when you felt God's presence and refer to it when you are feeling challenged, lost or despondent.
- Erase the notion of entitlement from every aspect of your life and receive God's blessings with humility and introspection.
- Focus on the needs of those who are struggling. You will appreciate your own blessings.
- Keep a gratitude journal and record a list of things for which you are grateful. Doing so will remind you of God's abundance and, at the same time, recognize God for his generosity and kindness.

BE GENEROUS

A transformed heart is a generous heart. You cannot claim to be transformed and walk in the new grace of God if you do not have empathy and compassion for those in need. Strive to be like Jesus who could feel people's pain and needs deeply. Generosity is not a one-off thing; it's a lifestyle. We serve a generous God who loves to give. As his children, we should follow in his footsteps. Prepare your heart for a lifetime of generosity.

> *"Remember this: Whoever sows sparingly will also reap sparingly, and whoever sows generously will also reap generously."*
> 2 CORINTHIANS 9:6 NIV

Ways To Practice Generosity:

- Be generous with your time. Volunteer, play with your kids, and give your undivided attention to people who will benefit from your attention.
- Be generous with your words. Give compliments, praise and encouragement. Be inspired by Barnabas from Acts 11: 22-26. Words of kindness cost you nothing.

- Share your skills and talents to benefit individuals and organizations that would not otherwise have the resources to pay for services such as tutoring, business consulting, legal advice, etc.
- Give away your worldly possessions to people who need them. You can't take it with you. (Matthew 6:19-20)
- Share your financial resources. God loves a cheerful giver. (2 Corinthians 9:7)
- Be generous with your grace and forgiveness. Let go of grudges you have against those who have hurt you. Forgive as you have been forgiven.

CHAPTER THREE

Living Consistently

We've all heard that a house built on a shaky foundation is in danger of collapse. But a house built on a solid foundation will stand, come wind or floods. We aim to build our Christian lives on a strong foundation of steadfast belief, but that doesn't happen by sheer luck. You must put in a consistent effort to make your foundation strong.

Before we delve into the measures necessary for living a consistent Christian life, there are some things to keep in mind. First, the Christian journey is not a 100-meter sprint. It's a walk—a slow, steady push toward your goal of spiritual transformation. God does not expect you to have it figured out all at once.

In 1 Corinthians 3:2 (NIV), he makes that clear.

> *"I gave you milk, not solid food, for you were not yet ready for it ..."*

God knows exactly where you are in your journey and is patient and gracious enough to accommodate your growth from its infancy to full maturity.

Your Christian life will be filled with the same challenges as your secular life. It is easy to wallow in your mistakes and give in to the temptation to let them define you. But your life is so much more than a single action. You are the sum of your collective actions, ultimately defined by the way you serve God by serving others. Your character is revealed in how you rebound from your indiscretions and in the effort you put into living in a way that pleases God.

Finally, the people around you play a vital role in your Christian journey and, hopefully, they are also guided by the word of God. These relationships enable you to make your Christian walk more rewarding and consistent.

Living Out Your Christian Values

The definitive guide for every Christian is the Holy Bible. There is no need to guess who we are supposed to be, what kind of life we are to lead, or the values that should guide us. The Bible gives us a clear indication.

> *"... but the fruit of the spirit is love, joy, peace, forbearance, kindness, goodness, faithfulness, gentleness and self-control. Against such things, there is no law. Those who belong to Christ Jesus have crucified the flesh with its passions and desires. Since we live by the spirit, let us keep in step with the spirit. Let us not become conceited, provoking and envying each other."*
> **GALATIANS 5:22-26 NIV**

The Bible tells us what the Spirit of God has planted in us. The fruits of the spirit have been placed in our hearts and with nurturing, their seeds will become mature fruit. This sacred fruit—evidence that we've given our lives to Christ—doesn't fully form in a day. It requires time and patience. A relationship with Christ will yield noticeable changes. You will falter sometimes but spiritual maturity comes when you embrace those moments and learn from them.

SHOW LOVE

When Jesus was asked about the greatest commandment, he said without hesitation that it was to love God. And that commandment, he said, is closely followed by the commandment to love your neighbor as yourself.

> *"Teacher, which is the greatest commandment in the Law?" Jesus replied: "'Love the Lord your God with all your heart and with all your soul and with all your mind.' This is the first and greatest commandment. And the second is like it: 'Love your neighbor as yourself.' All the Law and the Prophets hang on these two commandments."* MATTHEW 22:36-40 NIV

The common denominator in these two commandments is love. You can't obey the second commandment without obeying the first. The only way you can love your neighbor or yourself is by loving God first. God is the embodiment of love. His love, in both theory and practice, is our guiding principle. The Bible is filled with examples of God's love for us. He loved us while we were still in our mother's womb and while we were still sinners. He gave his only son for our sins. There really is no greater love than that.

When we are led by what is good, we will only pursue the things that are good. This translates into showing love to others and putting their needs above ours.

SOW PEACE

As Christians, we are the flag bearers of peace. We are a voice of reason and reconciliation and we should reject any form of disharmony. This doesn't mean we are doormats for people to walk over, but we must choose our battles wisely. There are some battles you must step away from if peace is to reign. Backing away from a battle may prove difficult, but peace is worth the effort. When you struggle, remember that you are a child of Christ, and you have been called to sow peace under difficult circumstances.

> *"Let the peace of Christ rule in your hearts, since as members of one body you were called to peace. And be thankful."*
> COLOSSIANS 3:15 NIV

BE PATIENT

We've been told, "patience is a virtue." As virtuous as it may be, it's not easy to practice patience. You can fight it, but in the end, patience is a requirement of Christian living. We must live in God's timing. He never promised us that our lives would be easy or smooth, but he did say that he has a plan for us.

> *"For I know the plans I have for you," declares the Lord, "plans to prosper you and not to harm you, plans to give you hope and a future. Then you will call on me and come and pray to me, and I will listen to you."* JEREMIAH 29:11-12 NIV

To experience the plans God has for us, we must be patient and trust his timing. Like all things that come from God, we can be assured that it will be flawless. God knows best. And in his time, he reveals his best to us. This is the reward for our patience.

BE KIND

It's reasonable to worry that people will take advantage of our kindness, but we should not concern ourselves with what others might do. Decide instead that extending kindness to others is our lifestyle choice. More than just holding a door for a lady or offering a smile to a frazzled cashier, kindness is a frame of mind. Kindness is an intentional way of life. Rather than waiting for an opportunity, seek out ways to extend kindness.

Jesus is the purest example of someone who lived a life of intentional kindness. He searched for those in need and never turned away those who came to him of their own accord. For Jesus, kindness was instinctual. He traveled to lay hands on the sick, free of judgment and demonstrated great love. If we follow his example, love and kindness will go hand in hand. This means being kind to your neighbor, even as you love them. Regardless of ethnicity, skin color or political beliefs, everyone is your neighbor.

> *"Therefore, as God's chosen people, holy and dearly loved, clothe yourselves with compassion, kindness, humility, gentleness and patience."* COLOSSIANS 3:12 NIV

BE GENTLE

Imagine if Jesus had been more assertive in convincing people to believe in him. Instead, he chose a gentler approach. He respected others' beliefs. When questioned about the claims of who he was, he didn't throw a punch or make a fuss. Even when the Pharisees spoke ill of him and did their best to cultivate doubt, his approach was one of gentleness.

> *He answered, "Haven't you read what David did when he and his companions were hungry? He entered the house of God, and he and his companions ate the consecrated bread—which was not lawful for them to do, but only for the priests. Or haven't you read in the Law that the priests on Sabbath duty in the temple desecrate the Sabbath and yet are innocent? I tell you that something greater than the temple is here. If you had known what these words mean, 'I desire mercy, not sacrifice,' you would not have condemned the innocent. For the Son of Man is Lord of the Sabbath."* MATTHEW 12:3-8 NIV

As men, we tend to power up quickly when challenged. We must control our masculine impulses and respond with love, no matter how frustrating the situation may be.

People will question your beliefs, casting doubt on your conviction that Jesus died for your sins. Don't get riled up or respond in haste. Stop and take a deep breath. Remember how Jesus responded to the Pharisees? Stand firm, extend your love and speak truth with an attitude of grace.

EXERCISE SELF-CONTROL

A true test of character is in how we control our emotions, especially anger. It takes willpower, strength, wisdom and discipline to rein in anger and not act on it.

> *"Better a patient person than a warrior, one with self-control than one who takes a city."* PROVERBS 16:32 NIV

Self-control is a skill more worthy than any attribute of a warrior who conquers cities. Anger can be a blinding emotion. It prevents you from thinking clearly and can lead you to do or say things you will regret.

Contrary to our learned behavior, anger isn't an emotion of power, but a sign of weakness. The Bible speaks to how our anger makes us even more vulnerable to troubles.

> *"Refrain from anger and turn from wrath;*
> *do not fret—it leads only to evil."* PSALM 37:8 NIV

It's easy to succumb to misguided earthly standards, but it's essential for every Christian man to remember what is expected of him. These values are found in God's word and, if all else fails, we can simply live by Christ's example. When you stumble, remember that God's grace is available and always sufficient. You cannot live a life of consistency without God.

Tips for Living Consistently

At first, it may be difficult to adjust to the new life you are trying to achieve. How do you explain to lifelong friends that this is the new path you have chosen? How do you tell your spouse that you are working to become more Christ-like? When you slip into familiar bad behaviors, how will you deal with the judgment of people who are aware of your commitment to Christ? How do you get back on course?

When you're faced with a complicated situation, remind yourself that others have been in the same shoes. Proceed with confidence, knowing that those men made it through, successfully ignoring the naysayers and resisting the entrenched habits of a previously sinful life. A life in Christ is worth the effort and, in time, will produce the fruit you desire.

GIVE YOURSELF GRACE AND PATIENCE

Consistency does not equal perfection. It relies on the little steps you take to achieve a goal—in this case, your goal to live in a way that honors Christ. You will make wrong turns, fail sometimes, and trip over old habits. Give yourself the grace and patience you deserve. Practice does not make perfect; it makes progress.

> *"If we claim to be without sin, we deceive ourselves and the truth is not in us. If we confess our sins, he is faithful and just and will forgive us our sins and purify us from all unrighteousness. If we claim we have not sinned, we make him out to be a liar and his word is not in us."* 1 JOHN 1:8-10 NIV

God knows we are sinners. He knows we are imperfect. Yet, he accepts us. All he asks is that we confess all our sins to him, knowing he is faithful to forgive.

You will sin. You will make mistakes. But accepting God's unlimited grace should not be mistaken for taking God for granted. God sees our hearts and knows our thoughts. Any deliberate act of disobedience to his word equates to a rejection of his love for you.

> *"Jesus replied, 'Anyone who loves me will obey my teaching. My Father will love them, and we will come to them and make our home with them. Anyone who does not love me will not obey my teaching. These words you hear are not my own; they belong to the Father who sent me.'"* JOHN 14:23-24 NIV

You cannot claim to love God and then deliberately go against him. God knows those who belong to him. He knows where your loyalties lie and he recognizes those who truly identify as his people.

Honoring God means turning away from things that displease him. It's hard to overcome temptations that block your progress, but you can get back up and continue the race. You will remember who you are, who has called you, and to whom you answer. You will remember why you are in this race in the first place. You will remember the promised future God has in store for his people, including you. You will also remember the extraordinary, unending love that God has for you. You will move forward knowing his grace is available, and all you need to do is believe, receive and become.

> *"Yet to all who did receive him, to those who believed in his name, he gave the right to become children of God."*
> **JOHN 1:12**

At times we all feel burned out, discouraged or exhausted. Every Christian encounters situations that put them on the precipice of giving up. No matter how put-together and "on fire for the Lord" some may seem, it is not an easy journey for anyone. But God's grace is always within reach. You are not running this race on your own. You are not depending on or drawing from your own meager strength and abilities. You walk in faith with the help of Christ—it is neither by your power nor by your strength, but by the grace and mercy of God. Tap into God's grace by first asking for it.

It is OK to ask for help when the journey seems overwhelming. Accept the truth that you do not have all the answers. When you embrace your weakness, you become more relatable to others. Your arrogance is tempered by your human flaws. Admitting weakness is a strength within itself. Don't be afraid. Don't let your need to appear perfect get in the way of making progress. When you refuse to acknowledge your imperfections, you deceive others and yourself.

Every day will present new lessons for you. Your worst days will give you the best lessons. Don't be so distracted by your temporary misfortunes that you miss a valuable lesson. Your preoccupation with the "should have," "could have" and "what if" situations is a stomach-churning rollercoaster ride that goes on and on. Focus on what happened, embrace the lesson you can learn from it, and move forward.

Our unrealistic expectations fuel many of our struggles. Again, this journey is not a sprint—it is a slow, deliberate walk. Going from zero to a hundred is not as important as simply moving forward. There are no maps or step-by-step instructions for Christian journeys. Each one is incredibly personal and unique to the individual. Don't compare yours to others. Holding yourself to an unreasonable standard can rob you of the joy you'll find on the journey. Give yourself the grace to fail and try again. Take your time and practice patience.

When you do find success, celebrate your victories … especially the small ones. What you count as little can yield big results in how it encourages you as you head toward the finish line.

LET GOD INTO YOUR LIFE

In this journey toward consistency, keep your eye on the one you're trying to please: God. Seek to please him and live the life he has ordained you to live. But how can you hope to achieve this if you don't let him into your life? You must make room for God in every aspect of your life. A desire to live a compartmentalized life is not consistent with the relationship God wants to have with his children. He will not force his way in. He loves you too much to give you an ultimatum. God leaves the choice up to you. He has proven to you repeatedly that he wants to be in your life, but it's up to you to choose him. Salvation is a choice.

> *"Here I am! I stand at the door and knock. If anyone hears my voice and opens the door, I will come in and eat with that person, and they with me."* REVELATION 3:20 NIV

Jesus has the power to break down the door but notice what he does instead. He stands at the door and knocks. He isn't standing in the middle of a maze daring you to try your luck at finding him. He is literally standing outside your door, knocking and calling out to you. All you must do is open the door and let him in.

LET GOD INTO YOUR MARRIAGE

Marriage is an institution designed and ordained by God. At the start of your marriage, you went to the altar of God and made a vow before him and your loved ones to have, hold and cherish. For some couples, those vows have lost their luster. You may be struggling to hold your marriage together. The truth is, only God has the power to save your marriage.

> *"Haven't you read," he replied, "that at the beginning the Creator 'made them male and female,' and said, 'For this reason, a man will leave his father and mother and be united to his wife, and the two will become one flesh?' So they are no longer two, but one flesh. Therefore what God has joined together, let no one separate."* **MATTHEW 19:4-6 NIV**

God declared the finality of marriage in this scripture. He joins a man and a woman together and no one and nothing can separate them. God protects marriages. He oversees the joining and has the power to keep two people together. If he can do all these things, shouldn't he take charge of your marriage?

If you are grappling with your marriage, that discord could interfere with your Christian journey and your attempts to live with consistency. A life of consistency does not include constantly arguing with your spouse or living as strangers in the same house. God calls for love in your marriage.

> *"Husbands, love your wives, just as Christ loved the church and gave himself up for her to make her holy, cleansing her by the washing with water through the word, and to present her to himself as a radiant church, without stain or wrinkle or any other blemish, but holy and blameless. In this same way, husbands ought to love their wives as their own bodies. He who loves his wife loves himself. After all, no one ever hated their own body, but they feed and care for their body, just as Christ does the church—"* **EPHESIANS 5:25-29 NIV**

The love that God expects in marriage is the same love that Jesus has for his church. It's a love that is forgiving, accepting, and defies all odds. When this kind of love abides in your marriage, nothing will separate you and your spouse.

Letting God into your life means handing over your marriage to him. If you aren't married yet, you can bless yourself by praying for your future partner, committing this unknown person into God's hands, handing over your future union to him and asking him to guide you to the ideal partner.

If you found God after you were already married, you may be in a more challenging position. Your spouse may not be in the same place as you when it comes to spiritual matters. God doesn't want your marriage destroyed, and he doesn't want to make life difficult for you. Pray for your spouse, pray for her heart and her salvation, and pray for your marriage. Through God, all things are possible.

> *"Jesus looked at them and said, 'With man this is impossible, but with God all things are possible.'"* MATTHEW 19:26 NIV

GIVE GOD YOUR DAY

When you wake up every day, resist the urge to pick up your phone to scroll through social media. Before you get up and get distracted, speak to God first. In other words, before you let the world in, let God in. Thank him for the day that has already been made great by him and commit your day to serving him by serving others. Prepare to unlock the blessings God will provide.
The Lord is set to bless you every day. He will protect you from your enemies, no matter what form they take or how they plan their attack. Commit your ways into his hands, set out to do the things that please him, trust him and he will keep his promises.

> *"Trust in the Lord and do good; dwell in the land and enjoy safe pasture. Take delight in the Lord, and he will give you the desires of your heart. Commit your way to the Lord; trust in him and he will do this: He will make your righteous reward shine like the dawn, your vindication like the noonday sun."* PSALM 37:3-6 NIV

GIVE GOD YOUR CHILDREN

Your children are your future and, likely, the source of your pride and joy. You have sacrificed for them and put their needs before yours. Every parent wants to see their child succeed, live well and be happy. The best way to ensure this is by giving them to God. When you choose the path of righteousness, there are blessings promised for your children.

> *"The fruit of your womb will be blessed, and the crops of your land and the young of your livestock—the calves of your herds and the lambs of your flocks."* DEUTERONOMY 28:4 NIV

You should pray for your children. Pronounce blessings over them and their future and pray for the good and perfect will of God to come to fruition in their lives. Ask God to order their steps toward the life he has preordained for them. Pray that your children will listen to God's direction. Pray for the friends they have and the ones they will make in the future. Pray that the helpers of your children's destiny find them and that your children will fulfill God's plan for their lives. Pray for the people your children will marry. Commit their union into God's hands and ask God to direct them. Pray for your children's children. Pray for the family they will create one day and speak peace over it.

When your children are believers of the word, it makes it that much easier for you to live a consistent life. Do everything in your power to give them a firm foundation in Christ.

GIVE GOD YOUR MIND

It's easy to get carried away with popular patterns and trends determined by today's influencers who likely abide by no moral compass. Unfortunately, we get lost in the noise and lose track of the standards we should cling to. The verse above speaks of a renewing of your mind as a means of transformation. In this sense, the transformation involves aligning with God's will for your life, but this change does not happen overnight.

> *"Do not conform to the pattern of this world, but be transformed by the renewing of your mind. Then you will be able to test and approve what God's will is—his good, pleasing and perfect will."* ROMANS 12:2 NIV

You must choose to give God your mind and keep your focus on the things that please him. Contemplate his mercy and the undying love he has for you. Let him infiltrate your thoughts. It begins by rejecting the ways of this world and holding yourself to an uncompromised standard of godly living.

God has a plan and purpose for your life, and a destiny designed for you before we were born. You can visualize your destiny as a place—the terminus of your journey. When you use an online map, there are typically various routes to your destination. The most direct route for life's journey begins with surrendering to God.

ELIMINATE NEGATIVE INFLUENCES IN YOUR LIFE

Here's a fact: Not everyone you know and love will accept this journey you are on. Some will doubt you. There will be those who are counting the days until you move past this phase. Sadly, there may be a few who want you to fail spectacularly. They will try to drag you back into the evil ways of this world. How do you deal with these people and eliminate their negative influence over your life?

This isn't a battle against faceless strangers. This is a battle against people who know you, love you, and may have been there for you through your toughest times. Walking away and cutting ties with them isn't your first or most inviting option.

It's up to you to establish boundaries. Draw a clear line between who you were in the past and who you are now and let your detractors see that line as clearly as possible. If they care about you as much as they claim, they will respect your boundaries. They may question your motives and may not understand your sudden pivot, but if they love you, they'll respect your efforts to pursue something better.

Establish boundaries that will help you avoid the things that get you in trouble. Think of these parameters as safety nets. Remember, you are on a journey to consistency. Although you're bound to stumble, setting boundaries on your own behaviors will help you avoid the temptations that can derail your journey. If you know that alcohol triggers certain behaviors and that being with your old friends will tempt you to drink, give serious consideration to who you're spending time with. The rewards of your new life will require sacrifice.

"Watch and pray so that you will not fall into temptation. The spirit is willing, but the flesh is weak." MATTHEW 26:41 NIV

Surround yourself with people who will help you grow. Keep these people close and give them permission to ask you the tough questions. You can also learn from their experiences. Be vulnerable enough to share your struggles with them and seek their advice. Yes, salvation is an individual thing, but you need like-minded companions to support you as you grow in faith. We aren't designed to do this on our own.

No matter what, only believe what God says about you and tune out the opinions of nonbelievers. They didn't put the hair on your head or arrange your facial features; God did. Don't rely on other people to help you feel good about yourself. God thinks the world of you and that's the only assurance you need.

Create A Routine Of Positive Actions In Your Life

Routines can be difficult to stick to, even for the most diligent among us, but they are essential for becoming our best selves, living our best lives, and keeping our focus on what matters. Gradually, new routines become habits that require minimal effort.

Adopting a routine of positive actions may be difficult at first, but you won't struggle forever. Before you throw a bunch of new things into your daily routine, remember that the goal is to be consistent. This means your new habits must be feasible enough for you to keep up with. Think of them as an upgrade or adjustment to your current lifestyle rather than a complete overhaul.

If you want to live a life of gratitude, start each day giving thanks to God. As soon as you roll out of bed, say aloud the things for which you are grateful. It can be the same list every day or you can change things up. Try to keep the time you do this consistent. Studying the word of God can also be a meaningful addition to your routine. Start by reading a verse or chapter each day or select a daily devotional. Spending time in God's presence puts things in perspective and improves your day and life. God promises that if we study and obey his word, we will prosper.

> *"Keep this Book of the Law always on your lips; meditate on it day and night, so that you may be careful to do everything written in it. Then you will be prosperous and successful."*
> JOSHUA 1:8 NIV

Make a list of the things you want to start doing and slot them around the things you must do daily. There is no need to make your routine complicated. You can start small and keep it simple. Take one new action at a time and focus on getting that one thing accomplished daily. Be patient. If you're like the rest of us, you'll go off track in the early stages of this change. The important thing is to get back on track instead of wallowing in your disappointment and abandoning your new habit.

MAKE ROOM FOR CHRIST

In Matthew 6, Jesus urges us to go to a secret place or room, shut the door to pray, and be in communion with God. This may not translate to an actual physical place, but rather a quiet moment in our lives when we set aside time for one-on-one interaction with God.

> *"But when you pray, go into your room, close the door and pray to your Father, who is unseen. Then your Father, who sees what is done in secret, will reward you."* **MATTHEW 6:6 NIV**

When you regularly spend time in someone's presence, you talk to them and learn from them, discover more about them, and maybe even act like them. When you spend time in God's presence, take the opportunity to gain a deeper understanding of who he is, what his will is for you, what pleases him, and how to become more like him.

Making room for Christ is vital to living a consistent life. When you're learning from him, speaking to him, hearing from him, and dwelling in his presence, it will be more difficult to stray from your Christian path or do anything that displeases him.

> *"Now when Daniel learned that the decree had been published, he went home to his upstairs room where the windows opened toward Jerusalem. Three times a day he got down on his knees and prayed, giving thanks to his God, just as he had done before."* **DANIEL 6:10 NIV**

We can learn much from Daniel. It's difficult to commune with God every day if the rest of our day is consumed with activities inconsistent with the values we proclaim on Sunday mornings or during our time with God. Living with consistency, the way Daniel lived, will align our Sunday morning life with the rest of our week.

Perhaps the best part about creating room for God is that we are assured that he'll be there when we are ready. There is no space or time that God does not fill with his presence.

TIPS FOR MAKING ROOM FOR CHRIST:

- Seek him and trust in his unconditional love. Accepting the love God offers allows you to diminish your own feelings of inadequacy.
- Recognize that God wants you to live in communion with him. God always wants you in his presence. This is why you should never shy away from speaking to him, even if you feel an overwhelming sense of shame. God is always ready to accept you.
- Allow God to soften your heart. You are clay and God is the potter. Make yourself and your heart available to be shaped and transformed.
- Simplify your life so you can make room for God. Make your time with God a priority and not an option.
- Spending time in God's word encourages you to open your heart and hear God's will for your life. If you're constantly feeding your mind and heart in this manner, his presence will be a constant.
- Memorizing scripture allows God's truth to take a more permanent place in your mind.
- Create a designated place in your home where you meet with God. It doesn't have to be anything formal or fancy. It just needs to be a place where you can experience God's love without distraction.
- Find people who will hold you accountable regarding your relationship with God. This is why the Bible says friendships are important, because when one believer goes astray, another draws him back.

"As iron sharpens iron, so one person sharpens another."
PROVERBS 27:17 NIV

SET GOALS

We all set goals, whether they are career goals, financial goals, fitness goals, etc. These goals remind us of where we started, keep our focus on where we're headed, and give us direction on our next steps. Setting goals is essential for our Christian journey. If we don't have a goal, how will you know if we're moving forward in our journey? How do we know if we are still on track?

Obviously, the ultimate goal of every Christian is eternal life, but there are many steps along the way. This is why goals need to be broken down into smaller parts.

Saying you want to live a consistent Christian life is an ambiguous goal. Your goals should be SMART. That is, Specific, Measurable, Achievable, Relevant, and Time-bound. Here are a few examples of smaller goals you can set to achieve the life of consistency you desire:

- GOAL: Read the Bible for 20 minutes daily for three weeks.
- GOAL: Listen to a 10-minute Christian-themed podcast on your way to work for four weeks.
- GOAL: Make a daily entry in a gratitude journal for four consecutive weeks.
- GOAL: Watch an online sermon from a church other than your own, twice each week for three weeks.

These goals are SMART, but you can make them even SMARTer by selecting activities that better align with your life and support the pursuit of your core values. Personalize these goals. Becoming a better version of yourself requires more than a cookie-cutter approach.

Put your goals in writing, not only for frequent reference but also to create top-of-mind awareness. Once you achieve your smaller goals, increase the complexity and commitment of your goals to help you grow in Christ.

FIND ACCOUNTABILITY PARTNERS

It's tough to achieve consistency on your Christian journey, but it doesn't have to be lonely. Find an accountability partner or a group of partners. They could be the key to helping you live a more consistent Christian life. The Bible speaks volumes about the importance of having someone around you to life you up.

> *"If either of them falls down, one can help the other up. But pity anyone who falls and has no one to help them up."*
> ECCLESIASTES 4:10 NIV

When you feel stuck in a rut or like you can't keep up anymore, your accountability partner can get you back on track. He may intercede for you, act as a sounding board, or stand as a source of strength. Often, we are too close to our own problems and struggles. Seeing your situation through the eyes of a trusted friend is beneficial. If you are struggling and can't find the courage or strength to ask for help, an accountability partner or group will notice and can intercede and pray for the things you may not even know you need. You'll be amazed by the power of knowing that other people are praying for you and encouraging you along the way.

The concept of accountability partners is biblical. The Bible is filled with examples of these relationships, including Moses and Aaron, Paul and Silas, and David and Jonathan. These men lifted one another's spirits, supported each other, and held each other accountable.

> *"Therefore confess your sins to each other and pray for each other so that you may be healed. The prayer of a righteous person is powerful and effective."* **JAMES 5:16 NIV**

Effective accountability relationships are most successful when the following things are taken into consideration:

1. **Compatibility:** No relationship or partnership works without good chemistry and trust. Your accountability partnership will only be beneficial if you can work together.
2. **Honesty:** For an accountability partnership to work, both parties must be vulnerable and honest with each other. To make it work, the partners must have confidence and permission to speak with candor.
3. **Commitment:** All parties must put in the work and commit to a common goal. Sometimes, one person will be weak in their spirit and will need the others to lift them up.
4. **Trust:** You must be able to trust those who are with you on your Christian journey. We need others to provide perspective and speak truth into our lives. If we are authentic and vulnerable, we're going to share information that might normally bring us enormous shame. We must be confident that we're in a "no judgement" zone.
5. **Faith-based:** Remember that your Christian values are the common thread in your accountability relationships. Participants must be solid in their faith and have an earnest

desire to follow Christ. God's word should govern these relationships. All advice and guidance offered should be biblical and directed by the Holy Spirit, who dwells in all of us.

Make Consistent Living A Priority

Setting clear priorities and assigning a level of importance to each is the critical first step as you execute your plan for consistent living. Here are some other suggestions:

- Sort your priorities into these categories: 1) important but not urgent, 2) important and urgent, 3) unimportant but urgent, and 4) unimportant and not urgent. Tackle the ones that are both important and urgent first, although if you address all important goals and tasks at the appropriate time, you will keep urgency at bay. Don't fret over tasks that are urgent but not important, and cross out tasks that are unimportant and not urgent.
- Your priorities aren't carved in stone. Life changes and so will your priorities but pay attention to things that hinder you from achieving your goals. If something is no longer relevant to your progress, let it go.
- Don't try to change everything at once. Do one thing consistently and master it! Trying to tackle all your goals at once can lead to inconsistency and burnout. Approach your priorities one at a time and stay on course until you achieve what you set out to accomplish.
- Change the way you think about willpower. Eat the elephant one bite at a time. Take baby steps. Even the tortoise finishes the race. Just keep slogging along.

- Surround yourself with unsentimental coaches who will urge you to higher levels of performance.
- Use your time well. The seconds that tick away can't be recovered or stored. Time is a precious resource. Spend it wisely.
- Don't get wrapped up in guilt, anger or frustration. You will make mistakes. Make peace with that reality right now. What makes the difference is how you manage mistakes and move beyond them. Forgive yourself when necessary and return to your plan.

> *"Jesus gave them this answer: 'Very truly I tell you, the Son can do nothing by himself; he can do only what he sees his Father doing, because whatever the Father does, the Son also does.'"*
> JOHN 5:19

STAY FOCUSED

To achieve what you want in life, you must stay focused. The same goes for living a consistent Christian life. Don't let your gaze shift to worldly temptations. Focus on God and don't blink.

Avoid Complacency

One of the easiest ways to lose focus is to assume that you've got this in the bag and are well on your way to living a consistent Christian life. Resist the urge to get comfortable. Self-sufficiency is the lie that many believers have unknowingly swallowed … hook, line and sinker.

> *"So, if you think you are standing firm, be careful that you don't fall!"* 1 CORINTHIANS 10:12 NIV

TIPS FOR AVOIDING COMPLACENCY: SURROUND YOURSELF WITH THE RIGHT PEOPLE

- The people you surround yourself with can have a significant impact. They may help you find your destiny and God's purpose for your life, but they can also send you off the rails. The best people to keep in your company are those who bring you joy and a sense of purpose. Just as you should protect your heart, you should keep guard over those who have the greatest influence over the decisions you make in your pursuit of consistent living.
- Find community groups or people who share your core values.
- Reevaluate your personal circles and centers of influence. Make new friends. (But keep the old ones who align with your plan for growth!) Beware of miserable people who hate seeing others succeed. They may even be people who love you! Identify and eliminate any toxic relationships early on and minimize the damage these negative influences can bring.
- Surround yourself with friends who will point out your spiritual blind spots and discuss them with you. Knowing that they are acting out of love and concern will make it easier to take in their truth, even if it tastes bitter.
- Don't rely on technology to be your primary source of communication with others. Physically spend time with the right people, reading their nonverbal cues and body language, and studying the emotion in their eyes.

STRETCH YOURSELF

- Building anything meaningful takes ample time and effort. You must put in the work to see the changes you want. Here is how you can stretch yourself for optimum growth.

- Don't bank on the achievements of your past. Yesterday's success has little to do with tomorrow's achievements.
- Personal growth and self-improvement often take place outside your comfort zone. Lean into your fears and uncertainties and explore what's waiting for you.
- Keep learning. A popular truism tells us that the day you stop learning is the day you die. Learning feeds your zeal and connection to the rest of the world.
- Initiate difficult conversations when there is conflict or discomfort in your relationships. Address the "elephant in the room." Don't settle for appearances of perfection.
- Consider the merits of opposing viewpoints by challenging your own beliefs. This opens your mind to endless possibilities and gives you new and refreshing perspectives. You may choose to stand firm in your original beliefs but considering alternative stances builds your confidence in your beliefs.

EXPLORE THE FOUNDATIONS OF YOUR FAITH

While blind belief in God is what you aim for, you must be vigilant against wayward doctrines and false prophets. As long as evil exists, there will be those who want to confuse you and steal your confidence with misinformation and intentional lies.

> *"Watch out for false prophets. They come to you in sheep's clothing, but inwardly they are ferocious wolves."*
> MATTHEW 7:15 NIV

Just as you guard your heart, guard your faith and core beliefs and hold them to be true. This is why it is so important to know God for yourself and to know what his word says.

"By their fruit you will recognize them. Do people pick grapes from thornbushes, or figs from thistles? Likewise, every good tree bears good fruit, but a bad tree bears bad fruit. A good tree cannot bear bad fruit, and a bad tree cannot bear good fruit. Every tree that does not bear good fruit is cut down and thrown into the fire. Thus, by their fruit you will recognize them."
MATTHEW 7:16-20 NIV

EXPLORING THE FOUNDATION OF YOUR FAITH

- If you've lost your enthusiasm for your current church, visit a new church. Maybe a different perspective will nourish your soul and rekindle your spirit. Rather than giving up on church entirely, explore options that may be a better fit for you.
- A wise pastor once told me that when you feel as if you're no longer being "fed" by your church, it's time to start serving your church in a new capacity. Give it a try!
- If you've stopped going to church, give it another try. The pandemic set a new pace for the way we do life; working and streaming from home are the new norm. But worshiping in person with fellow believers who share your enthusiasm and love for God is an important part of the experience. God is everywhere and while it's true that you can hear him anywhere, his word also encourages Christians to gather. Go back to church and experience God moving among his people.

"... not giving up meeting together, as some are in the habit of doing, but encouraging one another—and all the more as you see the Day approaching." HEBREWS 10:25 NIV

- Ask yourself if you're in the right denomination. Are there doctrines and rules in your current denomination that make you feel uncomfortable and disconnected? Do you feel like you're being forced to serve God or that going to church feels like a chore? Ask an expert about the doctrinal or theological aspects of your denomination that confuse you. Once you have those answers, ask yourself if that denomination is still right for you. Feel free to explore other denominations but verify their faith, beliefs, and theologies. If you continue to be dissatisfied, don't rule out the possibility that you may have a "heart" problem instead of a "church" problem.

DO SOMETHING BIG!

Stoke the fire burning in your soul with some out-of-the-box thinking. If there's something you feel passionate about, start a movement and find others who share your passion.

> *"Be the change you wish to see in the world."*
> —MAHATMA GANDHI

In doing so, you will begin to discover new skills, talents and passions you never realized were within you. And when the going gets tough, be resilient. Don't give up! Stand by the things you're passionate about.

If you fail, that's OK. You'll learn from the experience and you'll work smarter and harder next time. Give yourself grace and anticipate better results the next time you try.

CREATING MARGIN IN YOUR LIFE

Creating margin enables you to choose where to target your energies and other resources. Margin is the gap between your current burdens and your capacity for additional work. It is a boundary that exists to keep you from burning out or losing yourself while attending to the needs of others. Giving yourself adequate margin allows you to stay focused on what is important. Humans, unfortunately, are not equipped with fuel gauges. It's hard to tell how much gas we have left in our tanks, but we can't run on an empty tank. Constantly giving of ourselves without taking time for ourselves is not a sustainable course of action. We must be intentional about creating margin because it doesn't happen automatically. Be intentional when it comes to protecting your needs, your space and your mental health.

Parkinson's law states that work expands to fill the time allotted for its completion. You must learn to effectively manage your time.

Tips For Creating Margin In Your Life:

- Learn to say "No" to anything that doesn't contribute to the achievement of your priorities and goals. It may not be easy at first and you may feel a degree of guilt but do it anyway. It will get easier and you'll be better off for it.
- Schedule "me time" on your calendar. Make yourself a priority and be OK with it. Spend time filling the cup for yourself that you are always ready to pour into others. Doing so will allow you to prioritize the things in your life that you value most.

FINDING BALANCE

Creating margin in your life and prioritizing your objectives does not diminish the importance of serving others. You must find a healthy balance between taking care of yourself and taking care of others. Here are some tips that will help:

- **Respect Your Own Purpose, Passion And Identity:** It is normal to care about the opinions of your friends and family, but there is a big difference between putting their opinions into consideration and letting their advice overrule your gut instincts. It's OK to ignore what others may say is best for you. You can always find truth in God's word.
- **Deal With Rejection In A Productive Way:** Rejection is painful but how you manage it doesn't have to be. Channel your energy into growing and healing properly. You have a purpose and promise ahead of you. Lean into your faith. Your joy is coming sooner than you think.
  Jesus was rejected but he ended up saving the world. Joseph's family rejected him and he ended up ruling over them. None of this was possible without God. He is essential for your healing journey. Cling to him and have faith that your rejection story will be turned around for your good.
- **Listen To Your Inner Voice:** We all have an inner voice. It is an instinct that alerts us in certain situations or an uncomfortable feeling that we can't shake off. This intuition also applies to your deepest desires and needs. It is the part of you that wants you to live your best life. Your inner voice urges you to live out your boldest dreams and it knows when you are burned out. It's in your best interest to listen.
  Another voice you may hear is that of the Holy Spirit. It is the voice of wisdom and truth. He knows God's plan for your life and his job is to guide you along the right path to your destiny. Whenever you are about to do something that is not in line with God's plan, he cautions you.

- **Fight For The Causes You Care About:** Stand up for your faith! Be unafraid and unapologetic when advocating for the causes that speak to you. Do not let anyone make you feel inferior for doing so.
- **Monitor Progress Toward Personal Goals:** We are saddled with myriad responsibilities to family, friends, employers, strangers and those less fortunate. This does not mean you should put off making progress toward achieving your goals. Take at least one step each day that furthers your personal aims.
- **Allow Yourself To Be Vulnerable In The Presence Of Others:** Showing vulnerability can be more healing and cleansing than you might imagine. Contrary to popular thought, it is not a sign of weakness. It takes courage to be vulnerable in the presence of other people. As you'll discover, the reward is great because it breaks down barriers and builds trust with those around you.

LIVE AUTHENTICALLY

Authenticity happens when your words, actions and behaviors begin to align with your core values. Revealing your authentic self seems risky when everyone else is only showing their best moments on social media. But remember that it is better to be content in your own skin and in your heart than to pretend to be happy for everyone to see.

To live an authentic life, you need both self-awareness and self-acceptance. Don't define yourself by what you see on social media or by the opinions of your inner circle. What are the genuine characteristics and values that define you? Who does God say you are? In what areas do you need to do better? Answering these questions helps you recognize your true identity.

Strengthen Your Willpower

To achieve any goal you set in life, you'll need generous measures of discipline and self-control. Your willpower must be made of steel to resist the temptations of fleeting pleasure that could jeopardize your long-term goals. Self-discipline is the bridge that links the goals you have defined to the goals you will accomplish. Without this discipline, you will never be able to tick that goal off your list.

Self-control, discipline and willpower can take different forms. It can be as basic as resisting temptation because you are focused on the goal of attaining eternal life. It could be turning down a second serving because you are trying to live healthier. It can also be fighting the urge to engage in an argument when you are being baited. The Bible links godliness to self-control. If you are in sync with God, it will be easier to stand strong and we have the word of God to guide us.

> *"For this very reason, make every effort to add to your faith goodness; and to goodness, knowledge; and to knowledge, self-control; and to self-control, perseverance; and to perseverance, godliness."* 2 PETER 1:5-6 NIV

Self-control allows us to spend less time preoccupied with destructive behaviors. It is not an absence of temptation, but a ready supply of willpower that gives us dominion over those destructive behaviors.

To increase your willpower, know your strengths. Understand your weaknesses and examine the parts of your life where you can improve, then work ardently to do so. Willpower does not equate to overconfidence. Even the strongest of wills can be broken. God's word tells us to take heed, lest we fall.

> *"So, if you think you are standing firm, be careful that you don't fall!"* 1 CORINTHIANS 10:12 NIV

Building your willpower does not happen overnight. Neither does it happen by accident.

Eliminate What Tempts You

Out of sight is out of mind. The best way to avoid life-complicating temptations is to avoid the situations that expose you to the vices you're trying to avoid. Whether you're trying to avoid junk food, alcohol or gossip, you can improve your chances for success by letting your friends and family know that you're making a change. Give them permission to hold you accountable. Be proactive in your efforts to facilitate meaningful change. Reacting to a tempting situation sets you up for failure and greatly reduces your chances for success.

Online pornography may be the most challenging form of temptation for men today. A recent study conducted by

OnlineSchools.org reveals staggering statistics about the use of online pornography. Study highlights include:

- 40 million Americans regularly visit porn sites.
- 70% of men between the ages of 18 and 24 visit porn sites at least once a month.
- 28,258 internet users are viewing porn every second of the day.
- There are more than 24 million pornographic websites on the internet today.
- There are more than 68 million pornography-related search engine requests each day.
- The average age when a child is first exposed to online porn is 11.
- The most popular day of the week for viewing online pornography is SUNDAY.

Sadly, the addiction to pornography is as prevalent among Christian men as it is in non-Christian men. A recent study by The Barna Group of college-aged males who were actively involved in campus ministries revealed that 89% of these men watched porn at least occasionally. A whopping 61% viewed porn on a weekly basis, and 24% of these college students viewed daily or multiple times per day.

Other studies have shown that sexual activity in males between the ages of 18 and 30 has dropped significantly in the last decade. Of those surveyed, 28% indicated that they had not had sex in the last year compared to just 10% claiming the same 10 years ago. Internet pornography has rewired the brains of young men in a way that has drastically reduced their desire for sexual intercourse. Many researchers believe that this is just the beginning of an epidemic that could permanently alter the relationships between men and women.

Pornography succeeds in creating unrealistic expectations in men's minds and causes them to lose focus—even when they are not watching it. A man may be randomly going about his day and the next thing he knows, his mind is replaying scenes he watched a few days earlier, distracting him from the task at hand.
The devil plays dirty with pornography, even causing these scenes to pop into a man's mind while he is praying. The whole purpose of his prayer is then defeated.

As men, we cannot fight this battle alone. We must ask God for help. Avoid being idle or alone at times when you would typically visit pornographic websites. Temptations and addictions must not to be ignored. Battle them with every weapon in your arsenal.

Experts who understand our addiction to pornography suggest that overcoming this addiction begins with the following:

1. **Practice absolute abstinence with pornography.** Treat pornography the way an alcoholic deals with alcohol. There's no such thing as reducing your exposure to alcohol or pornography. You must completely abstain. Once you go "cold turkey," your journey begins. One slip-up derails your entire effort.
2. **Understand the triggers that drive you to pornography.** Keep a journal that helps you identify the situations and circumstances that make you crave pornography. Once you understand that certain internet searches, driving through the campus of a local college, or walking by a Victoria's Secret store in the mall triggers these desires, adjust your behavior to avoid those situations.
3. **Utilize parental controls and content blockers on your electronic devices.** Admit that you have little control over the things that trigger your desires, then protect your heart and

mind from the images that could destroy your life. There's no shame in taking cocaine from a drug addict, and you should feel the same about your inappropriate sexual desires.

4. **Understand the underlying causes of your attraction to pornography.** Believe it or not, man's struggle with pornography has little to do with sexual release. In most cases, we are drawn to pornography because it replaces a sense of connection we want with other people. If you grew up in a dysfunctional home or were exposed to tumultuous relationships, you may have an undetected yearning for a healthy connection with other people. Once you understand the "why" of your sexual desires, you can develop a plan to keep these desires in check.
5. **Surround yourself with a support group.** You can't conquer this addiction on your own. There are too many factors that drive this destructive behavior. Unfortunately, you are incapable of recognizing many of these behaviors and the wounds that drive them. When you are given the opportunity to see yourself and your addiction through another person's eyes, you begin to break through barriers you never knew existed. Find an accountability partner or a support group that will advance your efforts to overcome this addiction.

Feeling Overwhelmed?

While our coping mechanisms may not be as strong as they should be, there are good solutions available when we're feeling overwhelmed.

1. **Break It Down:** As they say, the best way to eat an elephant is one bite at a time. Make a list of things that cause you stress

and divide those tasks into manageable action items. Identify small steps you can take today to remove this burden from your list.

2. **Talk About It:** Find another man with whom you can confide and lay it all on the table. Don't be ashamed to admit you're overwhelmed. Shining a light on your problems can be liberating. When you have the benefit of another person's perspective, it's easier to see obvious solutions that will make your life easier.
3. **Just Say NO!:** Stop obligating yourself to things that don't support your most important priorities: God, family and serving others. It's a commonly held belief that if you want to get something done, find the busiest person you know to help you. Don't be THAT person! Stay focused on systematically resolving the issues causing you stress.
4. **Take Some Down Time:** Setting work aside for a week or even a few hours can clear your mind and give you a fresh perspective. Add an appointment on your calendar for some "Me Time" and use that precious time to get away from the hustle, bustle and distractions you contend with daily.
5. **Create A Routine:** When we feel overwhelmed, a sort of paralysis can set in and keep us from getting anything done. Establishing daily routines keeps us focused and headed in the right direction. Even if progress is slow, it's still progress. Be true to your routine and don't let anyone disrespect it. Beginning the day in God's word is an ideal way to start. Before you let the world in, let God in. Also set aside time for exercise, quiet time, and reviewing your progress.

Unpacking Your Shame

Have you heard that little voice in your head telling you that you're not good enough or that you're never going to amount to anything? As hard as we try to ignore those messages, they are hard to escape and they bring plenty of emotional baggage with them. Those messages didn't get into your head by themselves. You probably heard those words from a parent, coach or some other influential person in your life. Once those seeds are planted, it's hard to prevent them from growing.

When we start to believe these words, even unconsciously, we trigger responses that are equally harmful. Many resort to alcohol or drugs to numb the pain. Some will withdraw from their emotions altogether. For others, it's a more outward response; we become selfish, aggressive, controlling, or we resort to bullying others to pay our pain forward. These deep scars of our shame can be destructive on many levels, and our efforts to mask our sense of unworthiness causes us to act out in not-so-flattering ways.

Even those who overcome their shame and find great success in life are haunted by something called imposter syndrome. Those afflicted by this psychological condition have persistent doubts about their talents and abilities. They have a deep-seated fear of being exposed as frauds. That's how damaging and resilient shame can be.

The best way to confront shame is by first acknowledging it. Taking control of the narrative playing repeatedly in your mind can mitigate the fear of that shame being exposed. Talking about your shame with a loved one or trusted confidant helps you separate your destructive inner monologue from the beloved child of God you really are. We need to see what we look like through the eyes of others and learn to recognize in ourselves what attracts them to us. This exercise will help us explore the root causes of our shame and neutralize those issues.

Erasing your shame begins with loving yourself. God doesn't make mistakes, and he specifically made you in his image. Cherish that thought and embrace the idea that you are, indeed, worth loving.

CHAPTER FOUR

4

The Road To Resilience

Resilience is an essential characteristic for any individual, especially for men wanting to embrace Christian values. The Bible speaks to resilience through various stories and teachings that encourage believers to persevere in the face of their greatest challenges. For Christian men, understanding resilience from a biblical perspective strengthens their character and deepens their faith in God.

Understanding God's Nature

Before you can build resilience, you'll need a better understanding of God's character and his desire for our lives. God is all-powerful and omnipresent; he is everywhere at once. He is all-knowing. He is faithful, good, just and merciful. God does not change. He is stable and consistent. He is our source of comfort and guidance. He does not make mistakes. Because of these wonderful qualities, we can place our complete trust in him with confidence that he has a good and perfect plan for our lives.

The best way to understand God's nature is to turn to scripture. The Bible tells us we can rely fully on God's wisdom rather than depending on our limited understanding. (Proverbs 3:5-6) We know God will direct us to what is best for us. For believers, God is our source of strength and protection. We can trust in him even in our most difficult circumstances. (Psalms 28:7) Finally, we can place our complete hope in what God has promised for our future, rather than dwelling in the misery of our current circumstances. (Romans 8:25)

> *"But if we hope for what we do not yet have, we wait for it patiently."* ROMANS 8:25

Growth In Suffering

Enduring hardship and emerging stronger is a prevalent theme in the Bible. A biblical perspective on resilience reveals that suffering, pain and challenges are not merely obstacles to be eliminated, but opportunities for growth and deeper faith.

One of the most recognizable biblical examples of resilience can be found in the life of Job. Job faced unimaginable hardships—he lost his wealth, his health and his family. Despite these overwhelming trials, Job remained faithful to God. While he expressed his doubts and frustrations, he clung to his belief in God's ultimate plan. Job's story teaches Christian men that resilience is not about denying our struggles but embracing them with a deepened faith. Job's example encourages all men to lean into God during tough times, knowing that he is our source of strength and comfort.

The Apostle Paul provides additional insight into resilience in his letter to the early Christians in Corinth. In 2 Corinthians 12:9-10,

Paul acknowledges his own weaknesses and how he found strength through God's grace. Paul's insightful perspective highlights that resilience can grow when we allow ourselves to become vulnerable with others. When Christian men acknowledge their limitations and depend first on God's power, they can overcome obstacles more effectively. Resilience is not merely about grit and determination, but about having humility and a steadfast reliance on God's support.

> *"But he said to me, 'My grace is sufficient for you, for my power is made perfect in weakness.' Therefore I will boast all the more gladly about my weaknesses, so that Christ's power may rest on me. That is why, for Christ's sake, I delight in weaknesses, in insults, in hardships, in persecutions, in difficulties. For when I am weak, then I am strong."*
> **2 CORINTHIANS 12:9-10**

The Bible teaches that trials can lead to personal growth. James 1:2-4 encourages believers to "consider it pure joy when they face challenges because these experiences produce perseverance" and strengthen character. These trials can help us cultivate patience, wisdom and a deeper understanding of God's ways.

In Romans 5:3-5, Paul echoes the wisdom of James when he writes that "we rejoice in our sufferings, knowing that suffering produces endurance, and endurance produces character, and character produces hope." This passage emphasizes that suffering is not an end unto itself but a process that leads to deeper faith and hope. Paul, who faced numerous times of trial and persecution, understood that each challenge he encountered strengthened his resolve and deepened his reliance on God.

His life serves as a reminder that suffering can transform our character and lead to a more profound sense of purpose.

The trials we face can refine our faith like gold in fire, refining and shaping us into more resilient individuals ready to face any challenge. Enduring such resilience fosters a sense of community, as we share our stories of struggle and triumph, encouraging one another in faith.

Psalm 34:18 reassures us that "the Lord is near to the brokenhearted and saves the crushed in spirit." This passage brings comfort and peace during tough times, reminding us that we are never alone in our suffering. Our challenges should push us to seek God more earnestly which, in turn, will lead to more spiritual growth.

Trusting God With Our Trials

Life is filled with hardships that leave us feeling lost and overwhelmed. From the struggles of adolescence and family issues to our personal failures in later years, everyone encounters trials. When this happens, we should turn to our faith. Scripture offers a clear perspective on how we can trust God in our difficult moments, reassuring us that we are never alone in our struggles. God may not take our troubles away, but he will always see us through them.

One of the key messages in the Bible about trusting God is found in the book of Psalms. Psalm 34:18 says, "The Lord is close to the brokenhearted and saves those who are crushed in spirit."

This verse reminds us that God is deeply aware of our pain and suffering. Instead of facing our trials alone, we can find solace in knowing that God stands with us, offering comfort and healing. The act of trusting God ultimately means believing that he cares for us even when we feel discouraged and lost.

The Bible encourages us to lean into God's strength during our times of trial. In 2 Corinthians 12:9, it says, "My grace is sufficient for you, for my power is made perfect in weakness." This teaching shows that our difficulties can lead us to more thoughtful dependence on God's power. When we recognize our limitations and surrender our fears to God, we open ourselves to receiving the full benefit of his strength.

Philippians 4:6-7 offers practical advice on how to manage our worries during trials. It says, "Do not be anxious about anything, but in every situation, by prayer and petition, with thanksgiving, present your requests to God." Here, we are encouraged to bring our concerns before God through prayer, emphasizing that a grateful heart can transform our perspective. Trusting God means actively seeking him, sharing our burdens and cultivating an attitude of gratitude, even in tough circumstances. Trusting in God leads us to a place of peace, hope and resilience as we navigate life's challenges.

Building Resilience Through Relationships

Relationships, particularly with other men, can play a crucial role in developing a stronger sense of resilience. The Bible highlights the importance of camaraderie, mutual support, and accountability, all of which can significantly enhance our ability to persevere and overcome challenges.

The relationship between David and Jonathan exemplifies a powerful bond that fosters resilience. In 1 Samuel 18, we see how Jonathan protected David from King Saul, despite the risk to his own status. This friendship provided David with emotional support and encouragement during a perilous time in his life. The Bible teaches us that God uses friendships to make us stronger. By surrounding ourselves with like-minded men who share our values, we can find encouragement when we need it most.

In Ecclesiastes 4:9-10, we read, "Two are better than one, because they have a good return for their labor: If either of them falls down, one can help the other up." This passage highlights the idea that relationships provide essential support. When men come together, they lift each other up, share their burdens and celebrate their successes. These relationships foster an environment where resilience thrives. When men embrace a posture of vulnerability and share their fears and struggles without judgment, it's bound to lead to a deeper connection.

Of course, accountability is crucial to nurturing resilience within relationships. Proverbs 27:17 states, "As iron sharpens iron, so one person sharpens another." In the context of male friendships, this means men are given permission to challenge each other on matters of faith and personal growth. The encouragement of other men builds our resilience. When we hold each other accountable to our goals and values, we create an atmosphere where personal and spiritual growth can flourish. Life's journey is complicated, but with the support of strong male relationships rooted in faith, we can face adversity with courage and determination.

Finding Some Sense Of Contentment

Finding joy and contentment seems to be an endless pursuit for many men. From a biblical perspective, this type of satisfaction is rooted in fully understanding your relationship with God and the principles presented in scripture. The Bible teaches us that true contentment comes from a heart set on God's purposes and not on external influences or material possessions.

The Apostle Paul provides a powerful insight into the nature of contentment. In Philippians 4:11-13, he says, "I have learned to be content whatever the circumstances. I know what it is to be in need, and I know what it is to have plenty. I have learned the secret of being content in any and every situation." This passage indicates that contentment is not solely about what one has. It's a mindset that is developed through faith. Paul's ability to find peace in both abundance and scarcity illustrates that contentment is a choice that starts with placing our complete trust in God.

You've heard it before, but God's word has always emphasized the importance of gratitude. In 1 Thessalonians 5:16-18, believers are encouraged to "give thanks in all circumstances." A grateful heart will shift our focus from what we lack to the blessings we already have. By recognizing and appreciating the goodness in our lives, we inherit a sense of contentment, even amid challenges. Practicing gratitude allows men to see the abundance around them rather than fixating on unmet desires.

In Matthew 22:37-39, Jesus emphasizes the importance of forging an impenetrable bond with God and other men. Building meaningful relationships brings joy and satisfaction that material things cannot provide. By investing time and energy into these relationships, men can experience deeper levels of contentment and resilience.

Proverbs 3:5-6 encourages believers to "trust in the Lord with all your heart and lean not on your own understanding; in all your ways submit to him, and he will make your paths straight." This submission to God's plan can lead to a profound sense of fulfillment. The process of aligning one's values and actions with God's will helps us discover our purpose. We can experience a sense of peace that transcends our circumstances.

Building A Resilient Spirit

Building a more resilient spirit involves drawing strength from our faith, community, and scriptural teachings. When men face difficulties, relying on the assurance that God is with them can alleviate fear and uncertainty. This foundation of faith helps us understand that every struggle has a purpose. God will use these experiences to construct more resilient spirits in his believers.

Cultivating personal character traits such as patience, humility and determination is essential for resilience. When men adopt a mindset that regards challenges as little more than a catalyst for personal growth, they can then embrace difficulties with a positive outlook. They can face future hardships with greater fortitude and confidence.

By looking to examples in scripture, such as Job and Paul, men can draw up a blueprint for living life with a resilient character. Ultimately, resilience is about trusting in God's plan and understanding that, no matter the circumstances, he is always present to guide and uplift his followers.
Building a more resilient spirit begins with trusting in God, creating community, and being intentional in using life's trials to spark spiritual growth. These steps will make us more resilient and can inspire those around us to do the same. Ultimately, these spiritual practices will equip us to navigate life's storms with courage and hope for a more resilient life.

My Encounter With Resilience

Over the last 15 years, many men have invested themselves in my spiritual development. It all started with a small group of four buddies who met weekly for the purpose of fellowship. Our gatherings were more about building relationships than studying the Bible. There were weeks when we'd go fishing, take a trip to the lake or just meet for a drink after work. We were all growing in our faith and struggling to lead more Christlike lives. We did life together. God was at the epicenter of our relationships and we became a band of brothers, unafraid to tackle any subject with each other.

Over time, our small group evolved into a more structured Friday morning Bible study that morphed into a group of 60 men. We became more committed to digging deeper into God's word and creating a space where men could be transparent, authentic and vulnerable with no fear of their confidence being betrayed or shared with anyone outside our group. We were intentional about encouraging our group to break into smaller groups and create more intimate conversations while building trust and camaraderie.

These men shared their testimonies, mentored younger men and navigated difficult challenges together. As a result, we grew in our faith and spiritual maturity. In true Ephesians 6-style, we put on the armor of God and prepared for the battle called life.

I never imagined that these men were preparing me for the most difficult challenge I would ever face.

The most difficult day in my life was May 23, 2023. That was the day that my wife, Melody, took her last breath and slipped into the arms of Jesus at 12:15 in the morning, following a short illness. We had been married for 30 years and she had beaten two brutal rounds of cancer in the three years before her passing. Left with a weakened immune system from the clinical trial that cured her cancer, Melody developed a rare lung disease that, in a few short weeks, took away her ability to breathe on her own. My sons and I were with her when her medical team disconnected her life support. We held her hands, rubbed her feet, and did our best to remind ourselves that she was going to a place where she would experience eternal joy.

My wife was only in her 50s when she died. She loved Jesus and led a Christ-centered life by constantly putting herself in the service of others. Just two months before her death, she won a silver medal in a Pickleball tournament. Unlike me, she took care of herself. She exercised every day, ate right and led a healthy, active lifestyle. My boys and I struggled to comprehend how this disease could take her and take her so quickly.

I was completely numb in the hours that followed her death. I felt like I had an elephant sitting on my chest. I fought hard to avoid the emotional tidal wave that was about to set in. My primary focus was on trying to help my two sons process the very unreal reality that they would be deprived of at least 30 more years with their mother. She would not be at their weddings. She would never be able to hold their children. She wouldn't attend her grandchildren's Little League games or play hide and seek with them when they came to stay for long weekends. Of course, I also felt cheated. Our plans for retirement travel, grandparenting, winters in Florida and summers in Colorado wouldn't be realized. It all seemed unfair. What was worse, I had no idea how I was supposed to respond to that moment. As a guy who frequently cries at movies, I was stunned that I could feel no emotion.

In the days that followed, we did our best to focus on our happiest memories of her. We didn't allow ourselves to feel the profound loss. We didn't contemplate anything beyond making it through the funeral. There would be time, later, to deal with our feelings.

As I prepared for her funeral, I went to a local flower shop to order flowers for what we were calling her "homecoming" and the "celebration of life." The owner of the flower shop had known my wife and me for 30 years. He was strong in his faith and was not ashamed to tell people about his love for Jesus. As we discussed arrangements, he paused momentarily and somewhat reluctantly said, "Fred, can I share something very personal with you that might upset you?"

I said, "I guess so. What's up?"

He said, "I had a vision the other night about Melody. Would you mind if I told you about it?"

I could tell he was reluctant. We had spoken previously about his prophetic gift but I wasn't prepared for what he was about to share. To calm his fears, I said with a somewhat measured degree of enthusiasm, "Of course. I'd be honored to hear about it."

He then told me, "I had a vision that Jesus came and met with Melody last week while she was still in the hospital. Jesus explained to Melody that her time on this earth was coming to an end."

Knowing this man as I did, I knew he was being completely authentic with me and that what he was telling me was the absolute truth.

He went on. "Jesus said to Melody, 'I know how much you love your boys, Melody, and I know you've led a wonderful and meaningful life here, and because of that, I want to give you the choice of whether you stay here or come to heaven with me.'"

I saw a tear fall from the corner of his eye. At the same time, my eyes welled with tears as I imagined the tenderness of Jesus sitting at the bedside of my beautiful wife.

He continued, "Jesus shared a vision of what Melody's life on this earth would look like moving forward and what her new life in heaven would look like."

As he was talking, I recalled some of the tough conversations we had with Melody's doctors in the days before she lost consciousness for the last time. They had recommended a tracheotomy and had told us that Melody's reduced lung capacity would make it difficult for her to walk again or function as she once did. Our only hope was a lung transplant, and so we transferred to a larger hospital a few hours from our home for a consultation. Because of Melody's recent experience with cancer, the doctors gently broke the news to us that she was ineligible for that. The heaviness of that news was heartbreaking for both of us. In a matter of a few short weeks, my wife had gone from being a healthy pickleball champion to being unable to walk or take care of herself. We couldn't comprehend it. Melody took the news hard. Within hours, she began to fade.

The owner of the flower shop continued to speak gently. "Fred, as much as Melody loved you and the boys, she took Jesus's hand and said, 'I'm ready to go with you, Jesus.'" It was her last act of complete selflessness, he said. "She wasn't going to be a burden in your lives. She got a glimpse of her eternal reward and she knew what to do."

The emotional void and numbness I had been experiencing since her passing suddenly came to an end. I stood there in the flower shop and cried as the owner put his hand on my shoulder, smiled, and said, "She's with Jesus, Fred. She's alright. Now you've got to take care of yourself and your boys."

Surprisingly, the tears that were flowing down my cheeks weren't tears of sadness; they were tears of joy. The heaviness in my chest lifted. I knew my sweet Melody had left a world where she would

suffer and had now received the reward she had dedicated her whole life to earning. I wasn't going to let the selfishness of my loss outweigh the good news of my wife's heavenly gain.
A few days later, we held Melody's Celebration of Life in the same church where we were married 30 years earlier and where our sons were baptized. It was an extraordinary time of reflection on a life well lived. Coincidentally, almost every person who attended her service commented on the magnificent beauty of the flowers at her service. I smiled because the flowers had a special meaning that no one else knew.

I'm not sure why, but I kept the story of my encounter with the florist to myself for several weeks.

After the funeral, my sons and I began seeing grief counselors to work our way through the loss. I shared my flower shop story for the first time with my counselor. I expected him to raise an eyebrow when he heard the story, but instead he nodded with a knowing confidence, acknowledging that he knew my wife's encounter with Jesus was most certainly the real thing.

I waited a little longer before I shared the story with my two sons. Once I did, I could tell they found comfort in hearing it. They, of course, already knew their mother had a special relationship with Jesus.

As the months go by, I find myself still working through the various stages of grief associated with losing my wife. My trust in Jesus and my full confidence that my wife is with him in heaven is allowing my heart to heal in unexpected ways.

I owe that confidence to my band of brothers who helped me to know and trust God long before I lost my wife. I have grown because of my suffering. I have found a sense of resilience in this season of my life because I trust God and the work he is doing in me. He didn't take my wife to punish me for my sinfulness. He took my wife because it was part of a much bigger plan for my sons and me and everyone who knew my sweet wife and had witnessed her daily walk with Jesus. For perhaps the first time in my life, God has my full attention. I'm eagerly awaiting, but more importantly, I'm patiently trusting in him.

> *"Trust in the Lord with all your heart and lean not on your own understanding; in all your ways submit to him, and he will make your paths straight."* **PROVERBS 3:5-6 NIV**

Being resilient is about so much more than mental toughness. Resiliency comes when we understand the true nature of our loving God and place our complete trust in his ways, his works and his goodness.

Tips For Becoming More Resilient

- **Be Positive:** Stay positive in your thoughts and emotions. This will help you see new opportunities when they present themselves. When your mind is clouded by negative thoughts, you are prone to pessimism and may miss the good things God is placing right in front of you.
- **Embrace Your Challenges:** What you resist persists. It is better for you to acknowledge your challenges and face them

head-on. Sometimes, the harder we work to overcome an obstacle, the larger and more daunting that obstacle becomes.

- **Learn From Your Failures:** Take failure as a form of feedback and a chance for personal betterment. The only way you utterly fail is when you allow a challenge to keep you down. Draw strength from God, then get up and embrace the lessons you've learned.
- **Be Convicted:** Find meaning in everything you do. If you don't know why you're doing something, it becomes difficult to continue on your path, especially when times get tough. When you have conviction in your heart, you will find the strength to move ahead.
- **Avoid Isolation:** Man was not created to be alone. God's word explains that there's strength in numbers. Give and accept support from those who are willing collaborators. The devil loves to draw us into isolation so that he's never outnumbered. When we're isolated and not accountable to anyone else, we are much more likely to engage in destructive behaviors like pornography, alcohol or drug addiction and self-pity.

A PRAYER FOR RESILIENCE

Most gracious and heavenly Father!

Thank you for your untethered grace and mercy. Thank you for loving us in the unconditional way that you do. Even in our times of loss, we can feel you drawing near. You are faithful. You are good. You are just. You are unchanging and you are our source of comfort and guidance. Help us to trust in you, God, and lean not on our own understanding. God, I ask that you be with every man reading this and help him to navigate the trials and challenges in his life so that he can grow in you. Heal our hearts, God, and deliver us from the things that come to seek, to kill and to destroy. We pray for these things in the name of Your son, our savior Jesus Christ. Amen.

CHAPTER FIVE

5

Honoring God

"For although they knew God, they neither glorified him as God nor gave thanks to him, but their thinking became futile and their foolish hearts were darkened." ROMANS 1:21 NIV

Man's relationship with God is complicated. We struggle to prioritize our creator, failing to put him in the right place in our hearts, minds and daily routines. We are distracted by the allure of modern-day false idols. Our unstoppable pursuit of wealth, status and material possessions has us focused on the wrong prize. Don't worry—God gets it. He is still a jealous God, be He will be patient as we grow in our faith. He will be patient as we grow in our faith.

God has loved us since the beginning of time, countless ages before we were born. He loves us even though we are sinners. He still loves us when we repeat the same sins for which we previously sought repentance. God sent his only son to die for our sins and make us worthy of eternal life. God gives us hope. He gives us grace. He gives us the gift of his tender mercies when we least deserve them. He loves us, protects us, and guides us every second of the day. It seems only appropriate that we should honor God in all that we do.

We honor God by recognizing him as the creator of his kingdom and master of the universe. We can show him respect and gratitude through our words and service to others.

As men, we have endless opportunities to honor God. Rather than compartmentalizing our lives and creating one small box for our relationship with God, we should make room for God in every compartment, including in our roles as husbands, fathers and leaders. God is present in every part of our lives. It is only fitting that we honor him in all that we do.

How A Man Honors God

A man who wants to honor God does so by putting God first in everything he does. He fears God, but not in the way we traditionally understand fear. He is awestruck by God's magnificence and divine power. For that reason, a godly man does not want to disappoint God. His first inclination should be to seek God and let him be the epicenter of his existence. He should surrender his own will, making God the king of his life and willing to be led by the Holy Spirit.

Honoring God means putting God in front of all other concerns and needs. We should be eager to learn everything we can about God and to be diligent in our faith as we face life's trials. Next comes our service to others. We are to act with integrity and value the hard work required to support our families and serve God's kingdom. Humility should be a defining characteristic of a Christian man. We must be selfless, putting the needs of all others before our own. We should be humble enough to take the last scrap of bread and the last sip of water after others have been served. Honoring God means vigilantly protecting our hearts and overcoming the temptations that lead us to lust, greed, anger and all other sin. We must be intentional in resisting sin because God hates sin.

Showing gratitude for our blessings honors God. When we open our eyes to the work God is doing and has already done in our lives, gratitude comes naturally. Let's boldly express the joy we feel about the work God is doing in us and through us.

A man honors God by loving his wife as Christ loved the church, putting her needs above his own and working diligently to make sure she is happy, content, and confident in her husband's love. In the same manner, we must love our children unconditionally and bring them up in the way of the church, instilling in them a desire to know Jesus. As men of God, we must never withhold our love from our wives, children or anyone else, no matter how they have sinned against us.

We honor God through our generosity, tending to the needs of others and giving selflessly, even if the need is not obvious. Honoring God means that we won't seek recognition or reciprocity for what we give. We will expect nothing in return. We pray that God receives the glory for our acts of generosity and kindness.

> *"Now he who supplies seed to the sower and bread for food will also supply and increase your store of seed and will enlarge the harvest of your righteousness. You will be enriched in every way so that you can be generous on every occasion, and through us your generosity will result in thanksgiving to God."*
> **2 CORINTHIANS 9:10-11 NIV**

A man who honors God recognizes his responsibility to step up and lead when life's circumstances call for it. In leading, he not only encourages others, but builds them up by serving them in sacrificial ways. A godly man leads by example and allows his actions to speak louder than his words.

Even on his most challenging days, a man with a heart for God works hard to sow peace. When facing adversaries, he is authentic, transparent and genuine in his dealings. A godly man will do all he can to build a community of believers who will share in both the work and the harvest.

Honoring God Through Our Work

As men, we tend to compartmentalize our lives. To maintain a sense of order, we separate what happens at the office from what happens at home. The same is true for our spiritual lives. We don't like the accountability that comes with being the same guy on Friday evening as we are on Sunday morning. We may give our best effort in both our spiritual endeavors and our professional pursuits, but we are reluctant to merge the two and live consistently in every situation.

Unfortunately, we often let work define us as men. Our self-worth is deeply connected to our job responsibilities, the money we make, and our overall status with our employers. When we shift our thinking and recognize that our careers are only possible because of the gifts God has given us, we see the endless opportunities for honoring God through our jobs.

When a man accepts that his skills, experience, education, strengths, wisdom, talents and ideas are all gifts from God, it follows that he will want to use these gifts to serve and honor God. On its most basic level, work is a means of meeting our basic needs and caring for our families, but it has the potential to be much more. Let's look at our jobs as opportunities to build God's kingdom.

Your accountant may beg to differ, but in a very real sense, the money we earn belongs to God. The transactional benefit of getting paid for our work should be secondary in our minds. What if we viewed the primary purpose of our jobs as a means to build God's kingdom? Would we be more successful? Would our work be more meaningful? Would we jump out of bed on Monday mornings eager to serve God?

> *"Do not work for food that spoils, but for food that endures to eternal life, which the Son of Man will give you. For on him God the Father has placed his seal of approval."* JOHN 6:27 NIV

The bottom line is most men find life's purpose through their work. Wouldn't our work be more honorable if it revolved around serving God instead of paying the mortgage or buying groceries? Sometimes changing focus and aligning priorities differently can be the difference between surviving your job and loving your job.

PUTTING TRUE PURPOSE INTO YOUR WORK

> *"All a person's ways seem pure to them, but motives are weighed by the Lord. Commit to the Lord whatever you do, and he will establish your plans."* PROVERBS 16:2-3 NIV

Are you working in a job where you frequently ask yourself, "Why am I here, God?" If you believe that God does everything with a purpose, consider that God put you there for a reason. God also put your co-workers, bosses and customers in the same mix as part of a good and perfect plan. Embrace this reality and be more intentional about doing God's work within the circumstances you've been given. It's no accident that you are where you are.

One of the most effective ways to serve God through your work is to let your actions ring louder than your words. You'll be surprised by the impact that living out your faith has on those around you. But don't underestimate the power of words. Using your words to encourage and motivate your co-workers aligns well with your actions as a follower of Christ. Do your best to build others up and let your affirming words breathe life into every workplace situation, no matter how difficult or challenging. Integrity is essential for building trust. This is especially true at work where there are so many opportunities to cut corners or cheat the company out of a good day's effort. The values you model and the excellence you pour into your work are a window into your soul for your co-workers. The way you serve your customers, co-workers and bosses allows others to see how a Christian man conducts himself.

You can also honor God by building a sense of community at your workplace. When possible, bring other believers together with the idea of welcoming Jesus into your business. Imagine how your company's culture might change if more of your co-workers were believers and conducted themselves in a manner consistent with Christ's teachings. Start by hosting weekly meetings to pray for your co-workers, bosses and customers. Focus your prayers on those who need it most. Let others know you are willing to pray for any special needs or concerns they have. Not everyone will welcome your prayers, but the ones who need them most won't object to the gesture. Pray for those who have been transparent about their challenges. Pray for those who have expressed even the slightest bit of curiosity about your faith. Pray that your example may lead them to open a door to God's grace.

Honoring God in the workplace requires "baby step" discipleship. It won't happen overnight, nor should it. Start slow and be consistent. Let people see you in action and observe how true Christians behave. When you hear your co-workers' stories and challenges, demonstrate compassion, kindness and unconditional acceptance, which are the true characteristics of a Christian. It won't be long before you and others see the work that God is doing.

> *"Whatever you do, work at it with all your heart, as working for the Lord, not for human masters."* COLOSSIANS 3:23 NIV

HONORING GOD AS A FATHER AND HUSBAND

The ways in which we honor God may evolve with the seasons of our lives. Perhaps the most challenging time for a man is while he is establishing his career and simultaneously stepping into new roles as father and husband. Honoring God while navigating these important relationships reveals a man's mettle. As the head of the family, men have an extraordinarily important responsibility and can set an example for generations to come.

A God-loving family man makes a daily habit of praying with his wife and children. Some families gather for a prayer huddle before everyone leaves in the morning. It sets a good tone for the day when we pause for a moment and ask God for protection and clarity. This is a good time to pray for the needs of others and ask for guidance as we face the day's challenges.

A morning prayer huddle is also an excellent time to demonstrate priorities so your kids get a feel for what's most important in life. Your children will take cues based on how you stack the things you pray for. What you identify as your priorities will eventually become their priorities.

We should encourage our children to spend time in God's word every day. Let your kids see you and your wife reading the Bible together. While sitting at the dinner table, open the Bible and share a story with your children. It's about creating good habits that will give children a genuine thirst to know Jesus.
A family man honors God when he demonstrates strong moral values in front of his wife and children. It can be as simple as obeying traffic laws or waiting for his turn in line. But stay vigilant, because children absorb more from our inconsistencies than from our lectures about right and wrong. Children learn best from the behaviors we model.

One of the best lessons to teach young children is the value of serving and loving others. It doesn't have to be complicated: open the door for another person or rake the leaves in a neighbor's yard. Your kids will come to understand that serving others is a normal part of life. If you want to have some fun with your kids while teaching them about service, look for ways to perform random acts of kindness for complete strangers. You can plug a quarter into an expired parking meter or pay for a meal for the car behind you in a fast-food drive-thru lane. Your kids will soon discover the joys of giving and serving.

One of the best classrooms for teaching children about God is in the great outdoors. When children observe the wonders of this world, from the smallest of insects to trees as tall as skyscrapers, they feel the vastness of God's glory. As you help your kids discover these things, give credit to the creator. After all, only God could create something so magnificent and beautiful.

Finally, a good father and husband leads his family by showing them how to practice gratitude. Most of us live blessed lives and, as a result, we take our blessings for granted. Giving thanks for our health, our family, the roof over our heads, the communities we live in, and the three meals we enjoy every day can give us a renewed perspective on that for which we should be grateful. It's important for our kids to know that God has provided these things. Teaching our children to give glory to God is a healthy habit that will last a lifetime.

HOW A SINGLE MAN CAN HONOR GOD

On many levels, our society ostracizes unmarried men because there is a sense that men who are not married and have no children are not contributing fully to society or to God's kingdom. It's an odd belief for Christians who would otherwise cling to the belief that completeness comes only through a relationship with God.

> "*... and in Christ you have been brought to fullness. He is the head over every power and authority.*"
> COLOSSIANS 2:10 NIV

While statistics show that most men will marry eventually, there is a growing number of men who opt for long-term bachelorhood. If you've been married more than once, you may understand that sentiment better than others. But there could be wisdom in waiting; research has found that the most successful unions happen when couples delay marriage until they are more mature.

Yes, it is possible for single men to honor God. This can be an excellent season for men to become more obedient to God by focusing on developing an honest work ethic, getting their personal finances in order and purifying their minds. Channeling their energies into preparing themselves for their future mates is time well spent.

Rather than rushing into marriage, a single man should focus on becoming the right person before he focuses on finding the right person. Becoming the right person requires spending time on self-improvement, getting personal affairs in order, and mending damaged relationships with estranged family members and lost friends. When these lingering issues are resolved, a man can leave his emotional baggage behind. He can enter his marriage unburdened by habits and behaviors that could have harmed the fragile new union. If a man has addiction issues with alcohol, drugs or pornography, the best time to deal with those temptations is before he brings another person into his complicated life. Until his house is in order, a man should embrace loneliness and focus on fixing himself.

It is during your journey toward marriage when you should reconcile the fantasies of romance with the realities of life. No matter how much you love another person, your compatibility will be jeopardized if your partner's goals are not aligned with yours. You may lack spiritual common ground, have different aspirations for parenthood, or discover incompatible priorities for your professional endeavors. Every man loves sex, but an awesome sex life requires an awesome marriage. If you and your wife have different expectations about marriage, the sex is not going to be great for very long.

There are many benefits associated with being a single man and you won't lack for opportunities to serve and honor God during this important season of your life. Take your time, make conscientious choices for your career and finances and do some deep soul-searching before you take the matrimonial plunge.

HONORING GOD AS A COUNTER-CULTURAL CHRISTIAN

"If we don't stand for something, we will eventually fall for everything." These words are a great reminder of the wisdom found in God's word.

> *"If you belonged to the world, it would love you as its own. As it is, you do not belong to the world, but I have chosen you out of the world. That is why the world hates you."*
> JOHN 15:19 NIV

We are in the middle of a culture war where there have been deliberate attempts to move God out of our schools and public life. While God is being pushed out, ideologues are gaining a full-access pass to our children to promote whatever propaganda fits their narratives. Christians are under attack. If you're a follower of Christ, the naysayers of this world will call you an extremist or claim that you've been brainwashed and blinded by the tenets of your faith. Most of these efforts have been led by anti-Christians and nonbelievers who feel threatened by the promises of Christianity.

This opposition is a loud minority trying to pass off their views as the will of the majority. Once God has been extracted from the lives of our children, the void can be filled with evil ideologies including gender dysphoria, anarchy, socialism and other belief systems designed to misrepresent the goodness and magnificence of God's dominion over the world he created.

To contend with these attacks, Christians must begin standing by their convictions and acting in accordance with their beliefs. We must abandon our passive, laissez-faire stance and take a bold stand on behalf of Christ. Rather than compromising our values and surrendering to peer pressure, we must stand on the principles that align with our Christian beliefs. Speak up at meetings. Participate in the PTA. Run for the school board. Have courage—God is on your side.

The Bible gives us a great role model in the life of Daniel, who was willing to give up his life rather than compromise his loyalty to God. Because he refused to bow to the earthly king of Babylon in lieu of worshiping his heavenly King, Daniel willingly accepted the consequences of standing by his convictions.

> *"At the first light of dawn, the king got up and hurried to the lions' den. When he came near the den, he called to Daniel in an anguished voice, 'Daniel, servant of the living God, has your God, whom you serve continually, been able to rescue you from*

> *the lions?' 'My God sent his angel, and he shut the mouths of the lions. They have not hurt me, because I was found innocent in his sight. Nor have I ever done any wrong before you, Your Majesty.' The king was overjoyed and gave orders to lift Daniel out of the den. And when Daniel was lifted from the den, no wound was found on him, because he had trusted in his God."*
> **DANIEL 6:19-20, 22-23 NIV**

Standing by your convictions to honor God does not require you to stand on the street corner bellowing out the good news of God. Standing up for Christ means living in accordance with his Word and being committed to growing in the knowledge of Christ. The more we know about God's word, the more intelligently we can talk with non-believers and those who are critical of the Christian faith. The more we live like Christ, the more convincing our message will be.

No one wins an argument by insulting their opponents, yet that seems the only strategy available on social media and the 24-hour news channels. Instead, we should try speaking calmly and intelligently about our beliefs without condemning or judging others. If our critics can witness us living out our Christian faith through compassion, kindness and humility toward others, it will be hard for them to condemn us or our faith. We should be unashamed of the truth found in the gospel. For most people, we may be the only gospel they ever witness. There are millions of people in the world who will never crack open the Holy Bible or hear a single verse of God's word. What they see us doing will be the only understanding they have about Christianity. It's important to live intentionally with integrity while loving and respecting our neighbors.

AN AUDIENCE OF ONE

Taking a stand may jeopardize some of our closest relationships. We might lose friends, and we could lose influence with those who are uncomfortable with our public declaration of faith. In the end, we only need God's approval. We should live for an audience of one and strive to please God in everything we do. If God is with us, who can be against us?

CHAPTER SIX

Building A Strong Marriage

Relationships can be tricky. Even the most charismatic and charming among us have relationships that have failed. As fragile beings, we are ridden with a fear of getting hurt. The truth is, we are going about relationships in the wrong way. We are not getting God involved.

As Christians, we should seek God's guidance before we make decisions, and when it comes to decisions, relationships rank near the top of the list. Choosing the woman you want to spend a major part of your life with is not a choice to be taken lightly. Who better to influence that decision than the God who knows the path our lives will follow?

It is impossible to get things wrong when we involve God in our decisions. That is why choosing a life partner who loves God with all her heart should be a priority. If you pick someone who puts God above all else, she will never do anything to hurt you because someone who loves God fears him and obeys him.

This does not mean that any woman who loves God is the right person for you. God's designed path and purpose for your chosen partner's life must align with yours. The Bible says that two shall become one, and that includes your combined destinies. Finding someone who loves God and has been ordained to be your partner is the best assurance you can get for a marriage that will last.

> *"The man said, 'This is now bone of my bones and flesh of my flesh; she shall be called 'woman, for she was taken out of man.' That is why a man leaves his father and mother and is united to his wife, and they become one flesh."* GENESIS 2:23-24 NIV

Put God First

LOVE GOD FIRST, BEFORE YOUR PARTNER

At a very young age, my children learned this important lesson at their Christian summer camps: "God First. Others Second. Me Third." That's a good lesson for life, but an even more essential lesson for marriage. If you want to have a successful marriage, you must put God first. When your relationship with God is strong, everything else falls into place, including your relationship with your wife. Likewise, your wife must love God first before she can properly love you. When you both put God first, it will be easier to obey God's word, and that includes what he says about your obligations to each other in marriage.

> *"Submit to one another out of reverence for Christ. Wives, submit yourselves to your own husbands as you do to the Lord. For the husband is the head of the wife as Christ is the head of the church, his body, of which he is the Savior. Now as the*

> *church submits to Christ, so also wives should submit to their husbands in everything. Husbands, love your wives, just as Christ loved the church and gave himself up for her to make her holy, cleansing her by the washing with water through the word, and to present her to himself as a radiant church, without stain or wrinkle or any other blemish, but holy and blameless. In this same way, husbands ought to love their wives as their own bodies. He who loves his wife loves himself. After all, no one ever hated their own body, but they feed and care for their body, just as Christ does the church—"*
> EPHESIANS 5:21-29 NIV

Christ loved the church so much that he was willing to give up his life for her. You should love your wife in such a way that you would, without hesitation, give up your life in exchange for hers.

PRAY FOR EACH OTHER

A day should never pass that you don't pray for your wife. Pray for her as much as you pray for yourself—and even more. You are both part of an important union and, therefore, your wife is an extension of you. If it is well with her, it is well with you.

PRAY TOGETHER

The family that prays together, stays together, and that is a fact. Spend less time arguing and more time praying. This is essential, especially if you plan to start a family one day. You and your wife should be on the same page. Instead of spending energy working against each other, use that energy to address the problem that is dividing you and then find common ground. Seek God's wisdom to help you solve the problems that cause strife in your relationship.

STUDY GOD'S WORD TOGETHER

You both have the responsibility of helping each other grow in your relationships with God. Your Christian journeys are entwined because you no longer run alone. Study the word of God together. The Bible holds the answers to every question—including those about your relationships. If you both study the word of God, his wisdom will carry you through difficult situations. Pray for your wife through and through. Pronounce blessings on her and watch the blessings manifest in her physically and spiritually.

SERVE GOD TOGETHER

You two are now one. Work together to serve God. Sign up for the same volunteer shift at a food pantry or soup kitchen. Get involved in a couples' small group or ministry that allows you both to explore your relationships with God. Once you see your wife's heart for God, you will be inspired to be more intentional in serving God together.

Sacrificial Love

Marriage is complicated. As husbands, we pass through life's seasons and the love we feel for our wives may change from time to time. There will be seasons when we are angry, exhausted and frustrated by life's circumstances. There will be seasons where the joy is so overwhelming, it would be impossible to imagine going through life with anyone else. In sickness and in health, in good times and bad, our love is real, and it endures.

AGAPE LOVE

There are four different words for love in the Greek language and each describes a distinctive type of love. The love we should feel for our wives is known as agape love. Agape is the highest form of love because it heals and unites. It is the kind of love most often used to describe the love God has for his children. Agape love impelled God to send his only son to die for the world's sins. It is a transcendent and selfless love.

As men, we are called to love our wives sacrificially. In fact, we are called to love our wives in the manner in which Christ loved the church.

> *"Husbands, love your wives, just as Christ loved the church and gave himself up for her ..."* **EPHESIANS 5:25**

So, what is sacrificial love? What does it look like in your marriage?

Sacrificial love begins with putting the needs of your wife before yours, no matter the circumstances. What your wife needs to feel happy, content and loved becomes your singular focus. It requires you to do things that might seem counterintuitive, particularly when so much of our energy is consumed in simply surviving and getting ahead of the guy in the cubicle next door.

Loving your wife in this way requires significant attention and mind space. You express your love by showing empathy and listening, without judgment or interruption, to the things that occupy her heart and mind. Sacrificial love requires you to give freely of your time, attention and compassion to your partner without expecting anything in return ... not even her time or attention. Sacrificial love means adopting a mindset that there's nothing more important on this earth than your wife.

For most of us, this level of commitment requires a press of the reset button on life as we knew it. But no matter how daunting it may seem, getting started is actually easier than you think.

Start by setting aside a block of time each week to devote your full attention to your wife. Schedule this time on your calendar and eliminate the possibility of distractions by turning off your devices and spending time with your wife in a place where no one can interrupt.

During this time, listen intently to what she is saying without commenting or minimizing her concerns. If she tells you that she needs you to do something, do it without hesitation and be true to your word. Follow through on everything you promise to do.

During the conversation, you may hear things that hurt your feelings or challenge your understanding. Don't get defensive; let the words soak in. Save your excuses for another day. Investing in your marriage requires you to sow peace. Avoid the temptation to keep score or defend your honor. Your goal is to get a better understanding of her feelings and to see her worldview. Loving your wife in this way will change both of your lives for the better.

Sharing Responsibilities

For the first 20 or so years of our lives, we have a self-centered focus. Someone takes care of us until we can take care of ourselves, but we rarely think beyond our own needs. When we merge lives with another person, we take on the burdens of finding common ground and navigating shared responsibilities.

Before you know it, we're surrounded by piles of laundry and dirty dishes. Kids need to be fed. Someone needs to walk the dog and run the vacuum. In the 1950s and '60s, right or wrong, there was a clear delineation of responsibilities assigned by gender. The husband's role was to provide and protect. The wife's role was to nurture and manage nearly every domestic duty. Dad would mow the lawn and work on the car. Mom would clean the house and cook the meals. In the 1970s and '80s, the lines of responsibility became fuzzy; Mom went to work so the family could enjoy the spoils of "the good life"—a bedroom for each child, walk-in closets and ensuite baths, multiple cars, Caribbean vacations, and other "essentials" their parents didn't have but that this new generation of families couldn't live without.

Today's economic realities require most couples to share the responsibility of earning income. They often manage their hectic households by dividing the domestic chores. In a sense, husbands and wives have both become breadwinners and bread makers.

Even with clearly assigned duties, there can still be tremendous tension associated with the completion of these tasks. When conflict arises in your marriage, it is wise to resolve matters quickly. There will come a time when being "right" doesn't make you the winner. You'll learn soon enough that maintaining peace in your home is the ultimate outcome. It is always best to sow peace when you have that option.

TIPS FOR SOWING PEACE IN YOUR MARRIAGE

1. Don't criticize, condemn or complain about the way your wife handles her responsibilities. You have nothing to gain by critiquing her efficiency.

2. Be grateful for her dedication to your family and your life together. Appreciate her for her strong suits, remembering the reasons you first fell in love with her.
3. Find ways to work and grow together. Even though it may be her responsibility to cook dinner on a Tuesday night, offer to help and enjoy the time you spend together.
4. Don't keep score. There will be times when the work seems disproportionate or unfair. Don't become resentful or complain. Sooner, rather than later, the tables will be turned.
5. Leverage your differences for the benefit of your marriage. You've heard the term "opposites attract." Use your strengths to complement one another's shortcomings. When this happens, express appreciation for one another.
6. Honor one another in the presence of your children. Take a moment to praise or brag about each other's accomplishments and skills when your children are in the room. It will be an early lesson on the way loving spouses support and appreciate each other.

It's inevitable that you will have difficult days. These are the moments when you are more likely to mistreat or dishonor those you love most. If you're angry or frustrated, use all the willpower you can muster to avoid criticizing your spouse. Save it for another day, and when your mood has improved, you may opt to swallow those critical words.

Remember to love your wife the way that Christ loved the church. Focusing on loving her will protect her feelings and preserve your relationship.

A Common Vision For Your Children's Future

One of the greatest sources of marital tension is usually a difference in opinion on how children should be raised, disciplined and nurtured into productive adults. Both of you love your children beyond measure and want what's best for them, but there can be considerable disagreement on how to help your kids become the best versions of themselves.

Among the areas where parents most often encounter tension are:

- video game usage
- curfews
- bedtime
- nutrition
- circle of friends
- participation in sports
- educational pursuits
- discipline

If you make a wrong decision on issues like video games, sports, and bedtime, it won't be the end of the world. However, decisions about education, discipline, and friend choices can put your child on a trajectory that has a lasting effect. Pick your battles carefully. The war for your child's future is something you and your wife can win together.

The most important rule of engagement is this: Never express disagreements over parenting decisions in the presence of your child or anyone else. These matters are deeply personal and carry an immense amount of meaning and emotion for your spouse.

Once a child detects a difference of opinion, he or she will seize the opportunity to side with the parent who favors the direction most aligned with the child's preference. No one enjoys feeling outnumbered, and that tension can drive a wedge into your marriage. Always present a united front to your children.

Uncomfortable memories and emotions from our own childhoods can adversely impact our effectiveness as parents. It's human nature to want a happy life for our kids, and our instinct is to spare them the pain, disappointment, and rejection we experienced during our childhoods. In our efforts to protect our children, however, we may cause them to miss out on the realities of life that can shape and define them as they mature. If your child's first experience with rejection comes during college or early in their career, they will be ill-equipped to face the consequences and emotional toll in the "real world."

We often fly in like rescuers when our children encounter rough patches that are a normal part of life. Denying our kids the opportunity to fail is far more damaging than the failure itself. If you've never fallen off a bicycle, you'll never understand the risk that comes with riding a bicycle. Our earliest trials and tribulations provide valuable context for the challenges that will come later in life.

The best time for parents to get on the same page about raising children is before the child is born. If you still have the luxury of doing so, have a candid conversation with your wife about your individual expectations for your children and your roles as parents. Make sure your goals are aligned so that your child doesn't get caught in the conflict. In areas like this, it's best to over-communicate regarding priorities and standards. If you already have children, that conversation can and should still happen. It's never too late to get in lock step on your parenting plan.

The Hierarchy of Your Wife's Needs

Navigating a successful and fulfilling marriage can be filled with challenges. When either spouse feels as if they aren't being heard or respected in the manner they feel is appropriate, tensions can rise. As a man who understands that women are wired differently than men, you have to work hard to better understand her needs and how you can help meet those needs.

Here are the eight things your wife needs from you:

1. **Affirmation:** Your wife needs to hear you say that you love her, that you're proud of her and that you're glad she is your partner in life. The longer you've been married, the less likely you are to give your spouse this reassurance. If you're not saying it, she's not feeling it.

   ... "For this reason a man will leave his father and mother and be united to his wife, and the two will become one flesh."
   MATTHEW 19:5 NIV

2. **Your Attention:** It's easy to get caught up in the chaos of each day. We take a myopic view of the world and focus on the things that must get done before sunset. We tend to take those closest to us for granted. You must be radically intentional about setting aside time each day for your wife and children. Open your calendar and schedule a recurring

appointment with your wife. It doesn't have to be a long period of time, but your time with her must be free of distractions, electronic or otherwise.

3. **A Sense of Protection:** Your wife needs to know you will protect her from anything that might threaten her. Everyone wants to feel safe in their homes, but more than that, your spouse should know that you're looking out for her. Her sense of security may be physical, but it could also be financial or emotional. You must communicate to your wife that you are committed to protecting her, no matter the circumstances.
4. **A Listening Ear:** Our senses are bombarded in so many ways, and it's easy to become distracted. Our wives feel valued when we eliminate the noise and give them our undivided attention. They want us to hear what's on their minds and, more importantly, what's on their hearts. They want us to listen to their problems without trying to solve their problems for them. Our wives want listeners, not fixers.
5. **Nonsexual Affection:** Women like to be caressed and touched without the expectation of sexual intercourse. Your wife will likely find comfort when you give her a hug or put your arm around her waist. Though it may seem old-fashioned, she'll love it when you hold her hand. Physical contact is one of many ways to express your affection. Despite men's most vivid fantasies, women don't crave sex in the way that we do.
6. **A Sense of Complete Trust:** Our wives must know they can trust us. They need reassurance that they can confide in us without the risk of being embarrassed or compromised. Your wife wants to share her emotions with you without fearing that you'll use the information against her one day.

She needs to know that she can complain about your mother without worrying that you'll run blabbing to your mom. Share a sacred bond of trust with your wife and guard the confidences you share.

7. **Unsolicited Assistance:** It's obvious when the house is a mess, dishes are piling up in the sink, and the laundry hamper is overflowing. What may be less clear is that your wife is overcome by the demands of her day. There will be days when she is besieged by deadlines at work. She's juggling her appointments, kid activities, and social engagements. There may be a clear delineation in your household responsibilities, but nothing will make your wife more grateful than when you voluntarily step up to help with a chore without being asked. She may be suspicious of your attempts to lighten her load, but she will, nonetheless, be grateful. Expect nothing in return for your good deed, but don't be surprised if she chooses to reward you in a way you won't regret.
8. **A True Partnership:** More than anything, your wife needs assurance that she is not alone in her efforts to build a good life for your family. Life is so much more rewarding when you have a partner who wants the same future as you. When you work together toward a common goal, the joy and satisfaction that comes from the process is almost as rewarding as the actual accomplishment. A couple's confidence strengthens and their dreams become more ambitious when there is synergy in a marriage. Teamwork makes the dream work.

Communicating With Your Wife

In 1992, John Gray wrote the classic book *Men Are From Mars, Women Are From Venus*. The book became an instant *New York Times* bestseller because it delved into the key differences between men and women. Gray focused on how men and women communicate with each other and how that communication affects their relationship. The findings and conclusions in Gray's book were revolutionary for the time.

The truth is that men and women are wired very differently. When it comes to communication, men and women assign different levels of emotion to every spoken word. Just as complicated are the mannerisms, facial expressions, and nonverbal cues we broadcast without even knowing it. As a result, a conversation can get complicated before either of you utters the first word.

Here are a few tips for improving how you can communicate with your wife:

1. **Validate Her Feelings:** Avoid the temptation to ease your wife's concerns by telling her that her worries are silly or unsubstantiated. Hear her out. Strive to see the issue from her point of view. Your intention may be to put her fears at rest, but dismissing her feelings as invalid can put a harmful strain on your relationship.
2. **Show Appreciation:** Let your wife know how much you appreciate the time she spends with your children. Show her that you value the work she does to help better your family's financial situation. Express gratitude for the sacrifices she makes daily to make a good life for your family. Be sincere

and specific when you express appreciation. Be intentional in making your expressions of gratitude authentic and genuine. *"Husbands, in the same way be considerate as you live with your wives, and treat them with respect as the weaker partner and as heirs with you of the gracious gift of life, so that nothing will hinder your prayers."* 1 PETER 3:7 NIV

3. **Keep Other People Out of Your Marriage:** If you're frustrated with your wife or some aspect of your marriage, do all you can to keep those issues between you and your wife. Avoid the temptation to seek advice under the false pretense that you're just trying to understand your wife. Sharing your problems with outsiders is nothing more than a veiled attempt to build allies. Most importantly, don't share your troubles with your children or other family members. It's not fair to your wife when only your side of the story gets shared with people you both care about. If your marriage is at a point that it needs an outside perspective, find a licensed marriage counselor. Work with someone trained to spot the causes of conflict and direct you toward solutions.
4. **Let Go Of The Past:** Men are competitive by nature, and we have a terrible habit of keeping score in nearly every aspect of our lives. We all make mistakes. Perhaps your wife said or did something in the past that made you question how much you can trust her. If you decide to forgive and forget an indiscretion, stick by your decision. There may come a day when you make a mistake, one for which you find yourself desperately seeking forgiveness. The most destructive thing you can do to your marriage is to let a past mistake negatively impact your future together. Show the kind of grace and

mercy God has shown to you. That's all part of loving your wife the way Christ loved the church.

"After all, no one ever hated their own body, but they feed and care for their body, just as Christ does the church—for we are members of his body. For this reason, a man will leave his father and mother and be united to his wife, and the two will become one flesh." **EPHESIANS 5:29-31 NIV**

CHAPTER SEVEN

7

Become A Strong Father

Fatherhood 101

Shortly after my first son was born, a good friend in her late 70s said to me, “Fred, raising kids will be the toughest thing you’ll ever do in your life.”

At first, I thought she was kidding. I was incredulous and thought to myself, “What’s so hard about raising kids? You change their diapers, feed them, dress them and put them on the school bus. So what?”

By the time I became a father, I had graduated college, navigated the first five years of my marriage, and started a new business. I scoffed at the idea that raising kids could be any more challenging than those things.

If you’ve raised children, you know how naive I was. It turns out my older friend was right. Raising kids was the hardest but also the most important thing I have done. At the time, I did not know what I was getting myself into. It wasn’t long before my crash course in Fatherhood 101 would begin.

The fallacies men have about their responsibilities as fathers are driven by the experiences we had with our own fathers. As kids, we didn't know what our fathers were dealing with. Mostly, they made it look easy. As societal standards and gender-based expectations have evolved, it's fair to say that more is expected of fathers today than what our fathers experienced. We might remember Dad coming home from work, grabbing a beer out of the fridge and spending the rest of the evening watching television, while Mom fixed dinner, washed dishes, folded laundry, helped the kids with homework and got them ready for bed. My experience as a father was markedly different.

There's a different standard for parenting these days. Fathers carry their share of household responsibilities besides taking an active role in raising their children. When we compare our responsibilities to those of our fathers, we're probably setting the bar too low. Nothing against our dads, but things have changed. Our kids need us now more than kids have ever needed their fathers.

Some things have not changed. As fathers, we need to lead our families by example. Depending on their ages, our kids are like sponges in that they observe and absorb every move we make. If we use curse words, they're going to use curse words. If we need alcohol to unwind and have a good time, they're going to believe they need alcohol to enjoy life. Despite our best attempts to mask our inconsistent behaviors, our kids are wise to what we're doing. The first time your toddler decides to parrot one of your favorite words while sitting in church, you'll be convinced of the importance of parenting by example.

I was embarrassingly naive about the challenges of parenting. There's so much more to being a father than feeding your kids, changing their diapers, and putting them on the school bus. We must rise above the previous generation's standard of simply providing for our families, and elevate ourselves to the roles of mentor, coach, jester, soother, encourager, inspirer and teacher. The days of being little more than a provider and chauffeur are long gone.

10 Things Your Kids Need From You

1. TO BE SEEN

There was a time, not so long ago, when children were to be seen and not heard. They were something akin to the Von Trapp children in the musical *The Sound of Music*. They were to behave, be fastidious in their studies, and make an appearance when their parents wished to be entertained. Life, especially for children, is far more complex than it used to be. Though it's difficult to pinpoint the causes, our children have far greater needs than we did as kids. As parents, we must be vigilant in protecting our children from the external influences that lead them down the wrong path. Advances in technology and social media influence have added layers of complexity to parenting. Because of the moral decay in our society, we must be more attentive than our parents were with us.

Our kids should be acknowledged and made aware that they are more important than our cell phones, Netflix specials or other distractions. They deserve our undivided attention. Their well-being must be among our highest priorities.

2. TO BE HEARD

Listen intently to what your kids are telling you, no matter how trivial the subject may be. If we want them to share the important stuff, we're going to have to put up with the silly, day-to-day nonsense that seems so fascinating to small children. It's all part of parenting.

If you want your kids to make eye contact with you when they are teenagers, set an example by making eye contact with them when they are children. Take a knee, sit down or do whatever you must to get on their level and look them in the eyes. If you're distracted by your smartphone screen when they need your attention, you'll lose their engagement at an early age.

3. HELP PROCESSING THEIR FEELINGS

It's a confusing world for kids. There are so many influential voices competing for their attention. It's hard for most parents to comprehend the conflicting messages kids receive every day. My wife and I noticed that once we sent our kids off to kindergarten, we were no longer their sole influencers. They were now exposed to the views and values of peers, teachers, and playground chatter. If you've been putting off that talk about Santa Claus or the birds and bees, don't worry … someone on the elementary school playground has probably already covered it on your behalf.

There is such confusion about gender, race and social status these days, and our kids need a steady compass. They need their parents to help them sort through all the confusing and conflicting messages. If they've seen us live our lives in a consistent manner and if we've established a trusting relationship, they'll be more likely to rely on us to help them sort everything out. There will come a time when our teenagers reject most of what we say, but if they've learned the difference between right and wrong, they won't lose their bearings. As early as possible, instill in your children that they can rely on you to help them understand and process their feelings of fear, rejection, sadness and curiosity.

4. SETTING BOUNDARIES

Believe it or not, kids appreciate having boundaries. They may complain about a curfew or a dress code, but they'll know the rules of engagement before they begin to test their independence. Our kids don't want to be in charge. They don't need Mom and Dad to be their best friends. Our kids need room to roam, but they also need to know where danger lurks.

5. MAKING MISTAKES

Our kids can learn a lot from their failures. If they experience rejection or ridicule when the stakes are low, little harm is done. If we protect our kids from these very normal experiences while they're young, they'll have no idea how to process these feelings when they encounter them as adults. Let your kids fall. Then allow them to pick themselves up and dust themselves off. This is great practice for the realities of life.

My father often used a metaphor about giving me enough rope to hang myself. What I did with that length of rope was up to me. I could use it responsibly in a productive way, or I could use it to cause great harm to myself. The intended message was that it was up to me to do the right thing. Through trial and error, I would eventually figure out that my freedom as a young adult came with great responsibility.

6. CREATING TRADITIONS THAT HONOR THEM

Our kids long for a relationship with their dads that is unlike any other relationship. Your son wants to play catch in the backyard just so he can have some alone time with you. Your daughter wants a date night when she has your undivided attention. She wants to be the center of your universe, if only for a few hours. We have an opportunity to create special traditions with our kids and then we have an obligation to protect and honor those traditions for as long as possible.

These traditions come in many forms. Maybe it's letting your son be the one to put the star at the top of the Christmas tree every year. It might involve wearing a silly hat for a daddy–daughter tea party on Saturday afternoons. The tradition, no matter how small, must be honored and carried out in an intentional manner.

7. GIVE THEM A THIRST FOR JESUS

More than just dropping our kids off at Sunday School or just teaching them about Jesus, we should take one additional step and help create a deep desire for Jesus in their hearts. If we're not careful, we may lead our kids to believe that Jesus and God are just historical figures in the Bible. I was raised to believe that God kept track of every one of my sins. As a child, I didn't love God; I feared God in an unhealthy way. I wish I'd know that Jesus wanted to have a personal relationship with me because he loves me and, through the Holy Spirit, is actively involved and ever-present. I could have used a friend like Jesus when I was a kid. Our kids should be eager to know Christ. More than just reading the stories of the Bible to them, pray with them and teach them how to talk to Jesus. Introduce them to fun, Christian-focused activities such as vacation bible school and church camp. The more grounded their relationship is in Christ, the more likely they are to stay close to him when they leave the nest. Create a true yearning for Christ in your children and it could change your family tree for generations.

8. GIVE THEM FEEDBACK

If you believe in the power of positive reinforcement, you already know how important it is to celebrate even the smallest of victories in life. Some of us grew up in the era of participation trophies; you won a prize, regardless of how well you played the game. During my formative years, only the best of the best were recognized for their achievements.

Participation trophies set our kids up for disappointment when their individual performance really matters. Social promotion gives our kids an inflated sense of self-worth. As they mature and enter the working world, they are doomed to discover the correlation between effort, compensation and promotion. When a peer is promoted because of their outstanding performance, the person who won trophies simply for participating in a sport will find it unfair. The rules in the workforce are different from those on the Little League field.

When your child does something, either disappointing or exceptional, give them immediate feedback. If what they did required an unusual level of effort or skill, give them specific praise and let them know how proud you are. If your children have disappointed you, the feedback you provide should also be immediate but delivered with constructive criticism and a reassurance that, while you are disappointed in their behavior, you still love them and will help them do better.

9. ENCOURAGE THEM TO DREAM BIG

If you've read the biographies of the world's most successful people, you know some of them, when young, seemed unlikely to achieve any form of success. The most inspiring stories of great leaders start with the humblest beginnings. Being born into poverty, oppression or severe disability did not hold these individuals back from accomplishing great things.

These stories prove our children can pursue any dream, regardless of their personal circumstances. Often, the only thing holding children back is the lack of confidence they have in themselves. As parents, we can play a crucial role in helping kids dream big and aspire to achieve extraordinary things. Besides providing positive reinforcement and painting a picture of success for our children, we can help them visualize a future filled with phenomenal achievement.

10. BE THEIR ADVOCATE

Our kids are likely to face lonely times when they feel as if the world is conspiring against them. These are normal feelings but can seem overwhelming when combined with the emotional turmoil associated with hormonal changes. That's why it's important for our kids to know that we've got their backs, no matter the circumstances.

When our kids make mistakes, as they inevitably will, they need to hear that while you don't condone their actions or the damage they've done, you still love them. No matter how frustrated you may be, this is not the time to alienate your children. Let them suffer the consequences of their actions while still knowing that they are loved.

Protecting Our Children

I've worked extensively with young adults in recent years, and I've discovered that we're bringing up a generation of people who struggle with anxiety. Recent studies suggest that nearly 40 percent of adolescents battle an anxiety disorder. There's no clear explanation for this sudden increase among young people, but experts suspect it could be caused by the prevalence of social media and overly protective parenting. We've all experienced periods of anxiety, but it's hard to imagine living with a disorder that is so all-consuming. Those severe cases of anxiety will likely call for professional counseling.

I suppose the parenting skills of many Baby Boomers and Gen Xers could be to blame for this problem. As parents, we rushed in to spare our children from the pain and disappointment we experienced in our adolescence. We inadvertently denied our children a chance to create coping mechanisms and problem-solving skills.

It's natural to want to protect our children from difficult situations, but we have somehow forgotten that our own troubled times shaped us into the humans we are today. Through adversity, we learned about perseverance, toughness and hope. Why, then, would we want to deny our children the benefit of those same experiences?

As parents, we are inclined to fix our children's problems. If Johnny says he doesn't feel well enough to get up on a Saturday morning to deliver newspapers on his route, we step in to make sure he doesn't suffer any consequences for missing his deliveries. Instead of making him gut it out or face being fired from his part-time job, we deliver the newspapers while he sleeps in. Johnny missed learning a valuable lesson about life: If you don't show up for work, you don't get paid.

When parents become overly involved and controlling the lives of their children, it's called helicopter parenting. These hovering moms and dads may do a child's homework, complete chores their children failed to do, and intervene in conflicts with teachers, schoolmates, and coaches. They'll do anything in their power to spare their children the pain and discomfort that inadvertently come with having responsibility.

Quiz: Are You A Helicopter Parent?

Take the test below to see if you are a helicopter parent. Answer Yes or No to the following questions:

____ Have you ever completed your child's homework because it was easier than trying to get them to comprehend the subject matter?

____ Have you ever shielded your child from the consequences they might have experienced because of a bad decision they made?

____ Have you found yourself taking your child's side after he or she has been punished by a teacher or coach?

____ Do you find yourself praising your child and giving them reassurance because your parents did not provide you with that kind of emotional support and you're worried your child will feel sad or rejected?

____ Have you ever made arrangements for your child's social life because they didn't feel comfortable inviting a friend?

____ Do you find yourself intervening in a conflict your child is having with another child?

____ Do you feel reluctant to provide constructive criticism to your child because you're concerned that you will hurt his or her feelings?

____ Do you find yourself making decisions for your child because they feel anxious about making the wrong decision?

If you answered YES to any of the above questions, you're probably a helicopter parent. Despite your best intentions, you may be doing more harm than good in your child's emotional development.

Trying to take worry and discomfort from your children's lives reduces their problem-solving skills and ability to be self-reliant. Over-protectiveness fosters anxiety because children feel unable to navigate situations they find challenging on their own. When bad things happen to your children, and they will, they won't know how to deal with the setback. When children discover that they're ill-equipped to deal with their problems, they feel inadequate, and their self-esteem suffers.

Of course, we never intend to harm our children. We have the best intentions of giving them a better life than what we had. Coping with life's challenges doesn't rely on good genetics that are passed from one generation to the next. Learning to deal with problems productively is a learned behavior that comes from navigating hardships that are a natural part of life.

> *"Train up a child in the way he should go; even when he is old he will not depart from it."* PROVERBS 22:6 NIV

Healthy parenting means helping your children develop problem-solving skills and coping mechanisms, so they don't become undone by anxiety when life doesn't go as planned. As parents, it's our job to help our kids understand boundaries and set clear expectations for being self-reliant. By communicating honestly with our children, we can help them be prepared for whatever life throws their way.

Raising Sons Versus Daughters

While it is generally agreed that both sons and daughters should receive an equal amount of nurturing and should be subject to similar consequences for their behavior, there is little consensus on whether raising sons requires a different type of parenting than what is considered best for raising daughters. The differences between the two genders are enormous but the nature versus nurture debate continues.

Studies show that baby girls, in general, get considerably more affection than their boy counterparts, yet much remains unknown about the outcome of this affection imbalance. While girls tend to respond more to relationships, boys gravitate toward action. When it comes to discipline, girls respond to words while boys require a different approach. A gender-centric parenting approach may seem intuitive, but the bottom line is that boys are receiving counseling services at a rate nearly triple that of girls. One could conclude that our parenting strategies are not working for our sons.

For dads, parenting either sex can seem like a daunting task. We can assume that our sons will react like we did when we were their age. Because boys find action more compelling than words, we often have rough-and-tumble relationships with our boys. We can identify with our sons, but daughters are a different story.

For most guys, it's a struggle to understand girl problems. Girls are typically more emotional and seek reassurance that our sons don't seem to require. Girls want their dads to show a keen interest and to participate in their activities. Girls who feel the support from their fathers are reportedly more likely to develop confidence and strong self-esteem. In many ways, our daughters want the same things from us as our wives. They want our trust, our confidence and our unconditional love.

Need more motivation to improve your parenting game with your daughters? It is widely believed that women pick their life partners based on the behaviors modeled by their fathers. They will set their standards for romance based on the example you've set in your relationship with your wife. Boys and men will come and go throughout your daughter's life, but the one relationship that will dictate the quality of her adult life will be the father/daughter relationship she experienced in her youth.

Look alert, Dad. You're being watched!

CHAPTER EIGHT

8

The New You

Not everyone in your circle of influence will be happy about your Christian transformation. You may lose old friends who can't relate to the changes they see in you. You can understand their views because you've stood in their shoes and perhaps had the same skepticism about Christmas or doubts about the benefits of living an authentic Christian life.

When friends express confusion or disapproval, respond with empathy rather than defensiveness. Engaging in open and honest conversations about your faith can help bridge the gap. Sharing experiences that show how your faith has positively influenced your life may inspire more curiosity than criticism. Listening with an open mind to their concerns and acknowledging their feelings can also foster mutual respect and, hopefully, acceptance.

Treat your old friends with kindness and respect. Even if your lifestyle has changed, strive to maintain the friendships that brought joy in the past. Inviting friends to join volunteer activities or attend a church gives them a front-row view of your faith's positive impact. By being inclusive rather than alienating, new Christians can demonstrate that their beliefs do not diminish the value of friendship. That alone could bring your old friends around to your new way of thinking.

It might be in your best interest to avoid drawing attention to your transformation. Let your actions be more powerful than any words you express. Keep your head down, be humble and work at your transformation diligently and faithfully. Let your progress be between you and God.

There will be times when you become discouraged and lose confidence in the path you've chosen to follow. We all have been there. Sometimes a Christian journey is like taking two steps forward and three steps back, but nothing worth having is ever achieved without considerable effort.

Sometimes you may question why you've decided to follow Jesus. You may not fully understand what is expected and may be worried about the next step in your journey. You may encounter spiritual warfare because Satan feels threatened by your growth. You may find God's word to be complex and confusing. You may find it difficult to speak out when it comes time to defend your faith. Fear not. Even the most seasoned Christians struggle with these things, but they know they aren't required to have all the answers. Living consistently is a process. It's a journey. The more time you spend with God's word, the more confident you will be and the clearer things will become to you.

Seasoned travelers may tell you that the journey is worth more than the destination. For Christian men like us, the destination is eternal life with God and that is inconceivably greater than the journey. Embrace the journey but look toward the horizon, where the reward of heaven awaits.

Living a Christian life serves as a powerful testament to the faith you have adopted. Actions always speak louder than words. By embodying qualities such as patience, humility, selflessness and integrity, you can make a powerful impression on your friends. This authenticity can spark discussions about faith and encourage nonbelievers to explore questions about spirituality. Perhaps when old friends see the joy, peace, and purpose that faith brings, they'll reassess their initial judgments.

Don't underestimate the time it may take to win over your old friends. Don't let their negativity and doubt derail you. In moments of doubt, strengthen your faith by engaging with fellow believers to reinforce your beliefs and receive encouragement in the face of this temporary adversity.

Getting Started

If you're ready to be more than just a Sunday Morning Christian, there are several ways to get started. But the most important step is to get started right now ... not next week or tomorrow, but today.

We've all been there: we vow to begin a diet or quit a bad habit, yet we postpone the start date until next Monday or the first of the month or New Year's Day. We quit before we begin. We must set our minds on a goal and get started ... now!

Our purpose for living a consistent Christian life is to reach the end goal—an eternity with God in his kingdom. You may think the transition from this life to eternal life will be a long time coming, but God's word offers a different perspective.

> *"The time has come," he said. "The kingdom of God has come near. Repent and believe the good news!"* MARK 1:15 NIV

This is what Jesus proclaimed to everyone who listened. He said that the kingdom of God is near and much closer than we think. If you want to be a part of God's kingdom, you cannot afford to be noncommittal for even one more day. You may not understand the urgency, but do you want to be on the wrong side of such an important decision?

Getting started is easier than you think. In fact, if you've been paying attention you might have noticed that God has already begun laying the groundwork.

Pay Attention To What God Is Doing In Your Life

God is always with you but in this fast-paced world, it's easy to be so distracted that you do not notice his presence. God is constantly at work. It is through him that all things came to life and continue to exist.

> *"For in him all things were created; things in heaven and on earth, visible and invisible, whether thrones or powers or rulers or authorities; all things have been created through him and for him."* COLOSSIANS 1:16 NIV

Nothing and no one on this earth was placed here by mistake. After all, he doesn't make mistakes. He is intentional in all he does and has an individualized plan for each of us.

God's plan for us is a hopeful and prosperous one. There will be times when we find get ourselves into trouble and rather than reaching out to God for rescue, we grasp for other solutions. God knows we are weak and susceptible to doubt, but he is standing by to help. He will not allow any trial or temptation to come our way that he knows we cannot handle.

> *"No temptation has overtaken you except what is common to mankind. And God is faithful; he will not let you be tempted beyond what you can bear. But when you are tempted, he will also provide a way out so that you can endure it."*
> **1 CORINTHIANS 10:13 NIV**

No matter what season you're in—one of abundance or scarcity, success or failure, joy or pain—know that God is at work in your life. God is easy to find and is eager for you to discover him.

> *"'Then you will call on me and come and pray to me, and I will listen to you. You will seek me and find me when you seek me with all your heart. I will be found by you,' declares the Lord."*
> **JEREMIAH 29:12-14 (NIV)**

That's right; God wants you to find him. He wants you to ask probing questions about his plan for your life. He waits for you to open the door and invite him in. When you are deliberately looking for him, it's easier to take in the enormity of what he offers.

Get In Tune With God's Plan

FOCUS ON WHAT GOD IS DOING AND COOPERATE WITH THAT WORK

Assess the current state of your life. Ask God to reveal the lessons you should take away from this season. Fully surrender and let God have his way so his work in you can grow and bear fruit. There is no better life path. Do not be deceived by your selfish ambitions.

INVITE GOD TO TRANSFORM YOU TO BECOME MORE LIKE JESUS

The life that Jesus lived is a perfect example of a consistent life. Jesus never expressed doubt about where he stood with God. Despite various temptations (Luke 4: 1- 13), trials, and tribulations, Jesus's stand never wavered. He kept his focus on God and paid attention to everything God did in his life. When the devil offered him the world, he declined because he knew God had bigger plans. We should strive to be more like Jesus and put our faith in the promises God has made.

ASK GOD TO HELP YOU BE FULLY PRESENT IN EACH MOMENT

We never want to be in the same spiritual place as we were yesterday, but sometimes it's in our best interest to slow down and appreciate the moment we're in. If we hurry to move to the next big thing, we may miss an important lesson from God and a chance to grow in our faith. Endeavor to be fully present in each moment.

MAKE IT YOUR GOAL TO SEE GOD IN ALL THINGS

Being present in each moment allows us to witness God in our surroundings—the people we encounter, the places we go, and those things we might have once considered a coincidence. God has preordained every moment. He sent that person our way, took us to that place, and caused that thing to happen. Whether we recognize him is ultimately up to us. Ask God to reveal himself in every situation.

FIND MEANING AND PURPOSE IN SPIRITUAL STEPPING STONES

How did you get to where you currently are in your spiritual journey? What events or situations affected your journey? Are there lessons to be learned from these milestones? Did God use certain situations as blessings for you? Assessing every spiritual stepping stone and reflecting on how each impacted our lives will enhance our understanding of how God works for our good. Spiritual hindsight can be very revealing.

TAP INTO THE TRANSFORMATIVE POWER OF REST

I am sure you did not expect this to be on the list, but it is an important point. Sleep is a spiritual exercise. It is an expression of trust, knowing that God will care for us through the night. We close our eyes in faith that he will wake us up tomorrow morning. If we are sleep deprived, it's difficult to pay attention to what God is doing for us. Clear your mind and refresh your body so you can be healthy for the spiritual work ahead.

NOTICE THE OPPORTUNITIES AROUND YOU.

If we believe that there is a purpose in everything that God does, we won't be surprised that he has put us in a specific place at a specific time. God has purposely put us in proximity to people with needs we can satisfy. God leaves nothing to chance. When you learn to recognize the signs God puts in front of you and then respond to those needs, you'll get a better idea of God's purpose for you.

> *"Whoever is kind to the poor lends to the Lord, and he will reward them for what they have done."* PROVERBS 19:17 NIV

EMBRACE INTERRUPTIONS

God uses interruptions to change our perspective. Those disruptions should not remove our attention from God. He should always be the focus; everything else is in the periphery. Are those interruptions actually a teaching opportunity from God? Don't be upset by them but embrace them and seek meaning from them.

FIND PURPOSE IN YOUR SUFFERING

What is God preparing us to do? God does not allow suffering or trials to come our way for no reason. There is always a purpose in our challenges. Endure the pain and the inconvenience until the storm passes, and the storm ALWAYS passes. Be assured that there is a lesson to be learned or growth to be experienced from our moments of suffering. Embrace them.

> *"...weeping may stay for the night, but rejoicing comes in the morning."* PSALM 30:5 NIV

WATCH FOR THE OPPORTUNITIES TO SHARE HIS TRUTH

It is a privilege to share the word of God and support his ministry, but do not think for a second that we are the ones doing God a favor.

We should feel privileged to preach the gospel and support God's works. God is so mighty that at his command, the stones will rise to worship him. Instead, he has chosen you and me for this important task. Don't take this honor for granted or make him regret his choice.

> *"I tell you," he replied, "if they keep quiet, the stones will cry out."*
> LUKE 19:40 NIV

USE THE GIFTS THAT GOD HAS GIVEN YOU

God gives every one of his children a spiritual gift. He chooses each gift specifically for the individual and hopes we will use them to advance his kingdom on earth. Exploring our God-given gifts helps us discover aspects of ourselves that we never knew existed.

The Bible lists a variety of spiritual gifts and says that the Holy Spirit is the giver of all these gifts. It is by the same Holy Spirit that we put these gifts to use.

> *"There are different kinds of gifts, but the same Spirit distributes them. There are different kinds of service, but the same Lord. There are different kinds of working, but in all of them and in everyone it is the same God at work. Now to each one the manifestation of the Spirit is given for the common good. To one there is given through the Spirit a message of wisdom, to another a message of knowledge by means of the same Spirit, to another faith by the same Spirit, to another gifts of healing by that one Spirit, to another miraculous powers, to another prophecy, to another distinguishing between spirits, to another speaking in different kinds of tongues, and to still another the interpretation of tongues. All these are the work of one and the same Spirit, and he distributes them to each one, just as he determines."* 1 CORINTHIANS 12:4-11 NIV

To live a life of consistent righteousness, do not take a gift from God for granted. He did not deposit the gift in you without reason. He expects you to use it to advance his kingdom. Don't complain that you didn't receive a gift. Every person has received a gift from God. Nobody has been excluded. You may have to find your gift by asking God to reveal it to you.

> *"Each of you should use whatever gift you have received to serve others, as faithful stewards of God's grace in its various forms."* 1 PETER 4:10 NIV

Our gifts are not a means to glorify ourselves or serve our personal agendas. They are to be used in the service of others and to exalt God. Whenever we make use of our gifts to benefit others, we are serving God. Return all glory to God, both in public and private.

God has made his gifts available to us and it is our job to receive them as he intended. The word "received" is used 258 times in the New Testament. It is the idea of taking hold of something—to accept and take ownership. Regard these gifts as the treasures they were intended to be.

While seeking out our gifts and doing the Lord's work, we must bear in mind that receiving a spiritual gift is not the end game. The final goal is attaining eternal life. Making use of our gifts is a means to that end. Nobody's gift is inconsequential. We all play a vital role in establishing and furthering God's kingdom here on earth.

> *"Just as a body, though one, has many parts, but all its many parts form one body, so it is with Christ. For we were all baptized by one Spirit so as to form one body—whether Jews or Gentiles, slave or free—and we were all given the one Spirit to drink. Even so the body is not made up of one part but of many."* 1 CORINTHIANS 12: 12-14 (NIV)

Identifying Your Spiritual Gifts

You may have a general idea of your spiritual gifts, but you might also be surprised to learn that there are other gifts in which you excel. I suspected that one of my gifts was leadership because of my many years in business ownership and management. I was surprised to learn that I was also gifted at being an encourager. However, my biggest surprise was to learn that my most dominant spiritual gift is hospitality. Now that I think of it, it makes perfect sense but I would have never been able to identify that as my strongest gift before I took a special assessment that helped reveal my spiritual gifts.

Lifeway Christian Resources, one of the world's largest providers of Christian educational materials, offers a free spiritual gifts assessment tool. To access this resource, visit https://www.lifeway.com and search for "*Spiritual Gifts Assessment Tool: Discover Your God-Given Spiritual Gifts*" to download.

There are also many references in the Bible to spiritual gifts.

"We have different gifts, according to the grace given to each of us. If your gift is prophesying, then prophesy in accordance with your faith; if it is serving, then serve; if it is teaching, then teach; if it is to encourage, then give encouragement; if it is giving, then give generously; if it is to lead, do it diligently; if it is to show mercy, do it cheerfully." **ROMANS 12:6-8**

"To one there is given through the Spirit a message of wisdom, to another a message of knowledge by means of the same Spirit, to another faith by the same Spirit, to another gifts of healing by that one Spirit, to another miraculous powers, to another prophecy, to another distinguishing between spirits, to another speaking in different kinds of tongues,and to still another the interpretation of tongues." **1 CORINTHIANS 12:8-10**

"And God has placed in the church first of all apostles, second prophets, third teachers, then miracles, then gifts of healing, of helping, of guidance, and of different kinds of tongues. Are all apostles? Are all prophets? Are all teachers? Do all work miracles? Do all have gifts of healing? Do all speak in tongues? Do all interpret?" **1 CORINTHIANS 12:28-30**

"Offer hospitality to one another without grumbling. Each of you should use whatever gift you have received to serve others, as faithful stewards of God's grace in its various forms. If anyone speaks, they should do so as one who speaks the very words of God. If anyone serves, they should do so with the strength God provides, so that in all things God may be praised through Jesus Christ. To him be the glory and the power for ever and ever. Amen." **1 PETER 4:9-11**

God has likely bestowed more than one spiritual gift on you. After taking the survey, you will see that you have a strong aptitude for some gifts while other gifts may not be as dominant.

You will discover the degree of your giftedness in the following categories.

- Leadership
- Administration
- Teaching
- Knowledge
- Wisdom
- Prophecy
- Discernment
- Exhortation
- Shepherding
- Faith
- Evangelism
- Apostleship
- Service/Helps
- Mercy
- Giving
- Hospitality

Identifying Your Core Values

Once you begin to live a life that honors God, you will find the need to establish some sort of guiding principles by which you plan to live out your life. Taking the time to identify a set of core values that speak to your vision of the man you wish to become will give you daily guideposts and parameters that can help you make important decisions and choices.

Your core values define who you are as a person, how you live your life and the decisions you make. It takes time and self-reflection to identify your core values, but it's a crucial step in living a consistent life. If you do not stand for something, you will fall for everything.

Once your core values are established, making decisions becomes easier because the only question you must answer is, "Does this action or choice align with my values?" Everything you do falls into a predictable pattern of behavior. If you ask this question every time a major decision comes your way, your actions and decisions will become more consistent. Soon your decision-making process will feel innate.

Life experiences, your family of origin, and the things you've been taught all shape your core values. But, as a Christian, the most important influence on your core values is how well you model your life after that of Christ. Your values should not deviate from the word of God. If you're striving for perfection, avoid anything that is outside the example set by Christ.

> *"Do not be yoked together with unbelievers. For what do righteousness and wickedness have in common? Or what fellowship can light have with darkness?"* 2 CORINTHIANS 6:14 NIV

Your core values will evolve as you grow older. Your priorities will change, and your personal situation will change. One thing that must stay constant is that your values align with the will of Christ.

STEP ONE

You can identify the core values that you want to guide your life by asking yourself the following questions.

1. What causes am I passionate about?
2. What do other people tell me that I'm good at? Can I use these skills for the benefit of others?
3. Are there existing movements or causes that I can advocate for?

4. What are the traits I admire in the people I most respect? How can I emulate their actions and attitudes?
5. Where does the trajectory of my skills and talents intersect with my passion or what I believe to be God's purpose for my life?

STEP TWO

Explore this list of key attributes below, and identify those you believe best align with your vision for your future.

- ☐ Accomplishment
- ☐ Affection
- ☐ Affirmation
- ☐ Ambition
- ☐ Appreciation
- ☐ Authenticity
- ☐ Balance
- ☐ Change
- ☐ Clarity
- ☐ Collaboration
- ☐ Communication
- ☐ Community
- ☐ Compassion
- ☐ Connection
- ☐ Contentment
- ☐ Courage
- ☐ Diligence
- ☐ Diversity
- ☐ Encouragement
- ☐ Excellence
- ☐ Faith
- ☐ Family
- ☐ Father
- ☐ Forgiveness
- ☐ Freedom
- ☐ Friendship
- ☐ Generosity
- ☐ Gentleness
- ☐ Grace
- ☐ Gratitude
- ☐ Growth
- ☐ Happiness
- ☐ Harmony
- ☐ Honor
- ☐ Humility
- ☐ Humor
- ☐ Husband
- ☐ Impacting Others
- ☐ Innovation
- ☐ Inspiring Others
- ☐ Integrity
- ☐ Joy
- ☐ Kindness
- ☐ Leadership
- ☐ Learning
- ☐ Love
- ☐ Loyalty
- ☐ Marriage
- ☐ Mentoring
- ☐ Nurturing
- ☐ Obedience
- ☐ Openness
- ☐ Patience
- ☐ Peace
- ☐ Power
- ☐ Prosperity
- ☐ Purity
- ☐ Relationship
- ☐ Respect
- ☐ Risk-Taking
- ☐ Self-Respect
- ☐ Self-Reliance
- ☐ Service To Others
- ☐ Spiritual Growth
- ☐ Success
- ☐ Teamwork
- ☐ Trust
- ☐ Wealth
- ☐ Wellness
- ☐ Wisdom

Put a checkmark next to the words on the previous page that you believe align with the type of person you want to become. Which of these words reflect what belongs in your core values? For example, if you want to make a better effort to be more honest with your loved ones, you might choose the word "integrity." If you want to pick up a new set of skills to advance your career, you might select the word "learning." Place a checkmark next to as many words as you like.

STEP THREE

Now, narrow your selections down to your top 10 choices. If you have less than 10 attributes selected, go back and review the list again to make sure you didn't miss something that could be integral in your becoming the best version of yourself.

STEP FOUR

Once you've identifies your top 10, write a specific goal next to each of the ten characteristics you selected.

Here's an example of how your list might look:

1. HUSBAND: to be a more attentive husband.
2. ENCOURAGEMENT: to be an encourager to those around me.
3. FATHER: to be a more engaged father.
4. MENTORING: to be a mentor for a young person just starting his career.
5. OBEDIENCE: to be more obedient in listening to God's intentions for my life.
6. COMPASSION: to be more compassionate toward those less fortunate.
7. LEADERSHIP: to be a more proactive leader by setting an example for others.

8. RELATIONSHIP: to focus on restoring relationships that need my attention.
9. WELLNESS: to be more intentional about my physical and mental health.
10. GENEROSITY: to be more generous with my time and other resources.

STEP FIVE

As hard as it may seem, force yourself to narrow this list down to the five things you believe are most aligned with your values.

Your list of five might look something like this:

1. HUSBAND: to be a more attentive husband.
2. ENCOURAGEMENT: to be an encourager to those around me.
3. FATHER: to be a more engaged father.
4. OBEDIENCE: to be more obedient in listening to God's intentions for my life.
5. GENEROSITY: to be more generous with my time and other resources

STEP SIX

Next, create Core Values Statements using each of your five choices.

- **Example 1:** I will be intentional in encouraging other men in their walks of faith and in helping them navigate the various seasons and challenges in their lives.
- **Example 2:** I will strive to be generous in all things. Not just with my worldly possessions, but also with my time and attentiveness to those who need them most. I will not seek recognition or draw attention to my generosity on any occasion. I will endeavor to be generous when no one is looking.

STEP SEVEN

To pull this all together, you should consider your current investment of time and other resources that are not aligned with these core values. What can you do to rearrange your priorities?

> *"Yet you, Lord, are our Father. We are the clay; you are the potter; we are all the work of your hand."* **ISAIAH 64:8**

STEP EIGHT

Share your core values with your spouse and/or an accountability partner. Give them permission to let you know when you're not living up to your values.

CHAPTER NINE

Building Momentum

Once things start to fall in place, you'll want to do your best to keep moving your life in the right direction. You'll find that it's easier to build momentum in your progress when a multitude of things in your life start coming together as they should. It's hard work, but it won't be long before your forward motion is unstoppable.

Celebrating the Small Victories

Every small victory in your journey helps you become the person God intends you to be. The more you celebrate your minor victories, the more your faith will grow because you will see the endless possibilities with God. Celebrate all that God has already done in your life, including his gifts of family, friends, talents, skills, etc.

Acknowledging your small victories should give you a feeling of satisfaction because you are not where you were yesterday. You have hope that tomorrow you will not be where you are today.

Track your progress on paper. This gives you a physical scorecard and incentive to keep building momentum. Give yourself a gold star every time you hit a significant milestone. Take pride in your accomplishments and progress.

Outwardly, express gratitude for God's help with your progress. You experienced the taste of victory not on your own but with the help of the Creator. Give God the glory and adoration he deserves.

> *"Pride goes before destruction, a haughty spirit before a fall. Better to be lowly in spirit along with the oppressed than to share plunder with the proud."* **PROVERBS 16:18-20**

TIPS FOR BUILDING MOMENTUM IN OUR WALK

- Find peace amid your stress and anxiety. Close your eyes and take a minute to breathe and be at peace with yourself. Ask God, the giver of peace, to calm the storm in your soul so you can enjoy his unending peace.
- Treat difficult people with kindness and respect. The people you meet on your journey are there for a specific reason. Sometimes they are a blessing, but they may also be obstacles the enemy has placed to deter you from your goals. Regardless of their origin or intent, treat all people with kindness and respect.

> *"Whenever someone hurts you, choose forgiveness instead of retaliation. If God can forgive you for your sins, you can forgive other people for their minor indiscretions. The word of God declares that vengeance is the Lord's, so leave God to fight your battles and avenge you."* **ROMANS 12:19 NIV**

- Pray because you have a desire to pray, not because you feel obliged to pray. Prayer is not a chore to cross off your list. Pray because you want to talk to God and hear from him. Pray because you value the fellowship you have with God.
- Renew your mind with the truth of God's word. Thoughts become attitudes that ultimately shape you as a Christian. Your walk is not complete without the word of God. Meditate in his word day and night as God has commanded. Your mind will be renewed and transformed by this simple but important act.
- Embrace the grace and mercy that has been given to you and extend it to others.
- Find companions for your spiritual journey. The journey is long but it does not have to be lonely. You need others who will encourage you and share unbiased insight.
- Don't let shame push you away from God but use it to move toward him. There is no shame where God is concerned. His word calls you to come as you are. He has loved you since the beginning of time and that love is eternal.
- Ask God to help you learn from your mistakes. When you make mistakes and commit sins, ask him for forgiveness. Pray that your heart will be open to the lessons those mistakes have to teach.
- Be resilient. Your goals are not going to be achieved overnight. Dismiss the thought of immediate gratification or overnight success. Put in the work and be patient. Someday, you are going to experience the sweetest of victories.

FALL FORWARD

Life is a journey. We all lose our way and stumble from time to time. God's hand is stretched out to lift us up when we fall.

When we trust God, our relationship with him will deepen. God will renew what we have lost because of our failures and give us even more. Consider failure as a stepping stone toward what God has in store.

> *"... being confident of this, that he who began a good work in you will carry it on to completion until the day of Christ Jesus."*
> PHILIPPIANS 1:6 NIV

No faith journey is without some degree of failure. Anything worth pursuing has its share of challenges. True transformation begins when you respond to God's love by extending love to others. Love God with your entire being. Love yourself even though you are messy. And love others, especially when they are messy!

PUSHING THROUGH ADVERSITY

Make peace with your current circumstances. You may not like where you are, but your journey is unique to you. Adversity is an opportunity disguised as a barrier. Properly managed, it will lead to change that is for your benefit.

KEEP MOVING

Commit yourself to moving forward. Constantly complaining isn't beneficial and will only add to your sense of frustration. Expend that energy toward producing a solution. Go back to your core values and rediscover your purpose. With the blueprint of God's plan for your life in mind, you'll have the extra push you need to keep going.

Obstacles are strategically placed in your path by God to help you grow and develop the skills you need. The more you keep at it, the better you will become.

CHAPTER TEN

Creating A Spiritual Vision For Your Life

> *"For I know the plans I have for you," declares the Lord, "plans to prosper you and not to harm you, plans to give you hope and a future."* JEREMIAH 29:11

We seem to have a plan for everything we do. As you begin thinking about retirement, you create a financial plan. If you're watching your grocery budget or paying closer attention to your health, you put together a meal plan. If you're running a company, you probably have a strategic plan. Plans are an integral component of getting things done. We have contingency plans, operational plans, exercise plans and, sooner or later, a funeral plan.

As humans, we have a psychological need for certainty and consistency, and the best way to avoid stress and chaos is to create a vision, outline a plan, and determine the steps we will take to accomplish our goals.

Given our desire to know what the future holds, it's surprising that so few of us create a plan for the most important aspect of our lives: our relationship with God and the life he wants us to lead.

Creating a spiritual vision should be multifaceted and include plans for how you will serve God in all aspects of your life. Your spiritual vision can incorporate your marriage, your role as a father, education, career, personal finances, health, external relationships and, of course, your faith.

You must be intentional and focused to accomplish your spiritual goals. The best way to hold yourself accountable is to put your vision in writing. This allows you to monitor your progress and will remind you of the things you said you would accomplish. If goals are not written down, they are nothing more than good intentions, and we all know the road to hell is paved with those!

Getting Started

Before you begin creating your spiritual vision, take an assessment of your current situation. You must have a clear picture of your starting point before you can map out where you're going, but beware—our perception of the present can be shaded by issues such as an unstable marriage, substance abuse or wounds inflicted during childhood. Some of these issues will create obstacles in your journey. For that reason, it's important to work through your current challenges.

Changing your life for the better is important but it's never easy. This is going to take some work, determination and intestinal fortitude. Buckle up!

12 Steps For Creating A Spiritual Vision For Your Life

1. BEGIN WITH PRAYER

As with all major endeavors, it's beneficial to start with prayer. Invite God to guide you as you craft your spiritual vision. Ask him to reveal the areas in which you can improve. Why not clear the slate by first confessing your sin? Seek to understand the cause of your indiscretions and ask the Holy Spirit to change your heart and mind so you can be free from the sin that prevents you being your best self.

Let this prayer be a free-flowing conversation with God where you contemplate and visualize what you want your life to be. Pray for strength to remain steadfast in your pursuit of this vision.

2. STEP OUT OF YOUR COMFORT ZONE

The creation of your spiritual vision will require a level of self-awareness, honesty and candor that you may find unnerving at first. A spiritual vision, earnestly pursued, is nothing like a New Year's resolution where the promises you make to yourself are broken and abandoned within a matter of days. With a spiritual vision, you are thinking bigger and more ambitiously, considering things that once seemed outside the realm of possibility.

Fostering change in your life requires taking significant risks. Now, more than ever, you should be transparent and vulnerable in the presence of others. If you yearn for authentic change, allow others to have glimpses into your life that you've never shared before. Though the initial steps may seem frightening, every step forward will become easier as you learn to trust God more fully and those within your inner circle who accompany you on this new journey.

It's normal to be embarrassed about exposing aspects of your life that you'd like to change. Take it slow. Surround yourself with a group of trusted friends and mentors who understand your pain and support your commitment to change. As you let others into your life, you'll discover that nothing is more liberating than ripping away the veil and letting light shine on your troubles.

3. CONFRONT YOUR OLD WOUNDS

The amount of baggage we drag from childhood through adolescence to adulthood is astonishing. The psychological peril that was doled out in our families of origin and the unfortunate experiences from our youth don't fade. These issues don't magically go away; they simply lay dormant, waiting to emerge when we least expect them. Unprocessed trauma from our youth will affect our relationships for the rest of our lives.

If you ever wonder why some benign occurrence can suddenly make you angry or frustrated, it probably traces back to something that happened earlier in your life. If you wonder why you're feeling resentful, take a minute to consider the source of these feelings. The shame we carry can trigger emotions that may destroy our relationships with people who have no connection to our childhoods.

You don't have to be a psychologist to understand that the past actions of our parents, siblings, teachers and coaches can spark feelings of abandonment, anger or sadness. There are those among us who had our childhoods stolen because of another person's control issues, pride or sexual dysfunction. Decades later, a minor incident can trigger an outburst that is inextricably tied to a painful moment from the past. We lash out as if we are reliving a trauma that has been festering under the surface.

There's no shame in seeking counseling to help us sift through our pain. A counselor can provide context on how these long-ago events affect the way we feel about ourselves and those around us. No matter how composed or tough we may appear, we can't fix these things on our own.

4. SURROUND YOURSELF WITH GOOD PEOPLE

As men, we go through life with a false sense of security that we can take care of things on our own. We want the outside world to believe that we are undeterred. We don't allow little things to bother us, and nothing is going to get in our way.

When things become unmanageable, our fight-or-flight instincts kick in and, in most cases, we opt to retreat. It's tempting to slip into isolation, where we don't have to discuss our feelings or reveal our fears in front of others. When we move into isolation, we abandon those who might hold us accountable or ask tough questions. When we are alone, the devil has us all to himself. In this isolation, we are more apt to sin and engage in self-destructive behaviors like alcohol and drug abuse, pornography, and denying our love to those who need it most.

No matter how tough things may seem, we are not alone in our pain and troubles. There are thousands of men close by who suffer from the same insecurities and sinfulness as we do. Most importantly, there are millions of men who have walked a similar path before us. They understand what we're going through because they've been there themselves. They've successfully navigated the minefield. They can be a valuable resource.

Surrounding yourself with men who will walk with you through your trials can be your path back to joy. Best of all, God will bring these men to you. They are shooting hoops with you at the gym or sitting beside you at your daughter's dance recital. They're at church, in the office or at the family reunion. God will provide you with mentors and companions. There's no reason to do life alone.

5. CREATE A BOLD VISION

When you create a spiritual vision for your life, dare to dream big! You've heard Philippians 4:13 a thousand times, "I can do all things through Christ who strengthens me." That, my friend, is a check you can cash. When you think about your spiritual future, you should assume that nothing is impossible. Set your mind on the loftiest goal you can set.

What would your life look like if you achieved your spiritual goals? In what ways would that change your family? How might you change your community or the world? We should all go through the process of visualizing our success to understand that our dreams can become a reality. When you think of all the prayers and petitions you can take to God, asking for help accomplishing your spiritual vision is likely the most selfless request you will ever make.

6. SHARE YOUR VISION WITH OTHERS

You know from experience that when you set goals for yourself, it's easier to accomplish those goals if someone helps you keep track of your progress. You feel more motivated when someone holds you accountable for the self-improvement promises you've made. When you do something as important as creating a spiritual vision, you're going to want someone with you on the journey. The best companion is an experienced traveler who has already walked the road that lies ahead.

Be selective about your companions on this journey. You need someone who will guard your trust and encourage you. At times you will want to rest or even turn back. Your companion can give you the nudge you need to aggressively pursue your vision.

In addition to companions to keep you focused, you'll need a host of strategies to keep you on your path. Post reminders of your vision on the bathroom mirror, refrigerator door, car dashboard, or home screen on your phone or computer. From the moment you wake until you go to sleep, keep your spiritual vision front and center.

7. GIVE UP CONTROL

This truth bears repeating: one of our greatest shortcomings as men is our need to be in control … all the time. When we feel we're losing control, many of us will "power up" and get loud to prove that we're still in charge of the situation. That's often when God gives us a gentle reminder about who's actually in charge and who controls every atom in the universe. Although we still have our free will, it should be abundantly clear that God's in charge.

Because of the assurances God makes to his followers, we know we can lay any worry at his feet. When it comes to creating a spiritual vision, we can admit to God that "our way" hasn't worked out well.

Surrendering to God and acknowledging that we can't do life on our own is an important step in charting our spiritual course.

Perhaps you've heard the oft-quoted phrase, "Let go and let God." It's a valuable reminder that we must let go of our desire to call the shots and give control to God. He will help us shape a spiritual vision that pleases him and sustains us.

8. CREATE A DAILY HABIT

As you work through the process of creating your spiritual vision, take advantage of any chance to stop and contemplate what you want your life to be. Carve out a small portion of your day to be in communion with God. Read scripture and ask God to let the words on the page speak to you in way that will add meaning to your life and purpose to your journey.

You can find the answers you're looking for in God's word if you lower your guard, set aside your distractions and look earnestly for meaning. If you're a new believer, spend time in the New Testament book of James. In just five short chapters, you'll find guidance on living a life that pleases God. Don't just read it once. Read it over and over and the meaning will resonate with you in a different way every time you read it. The words haven't changed, but you, as a person, have changed since the last time you read those verses. You will continue to change, and God's word will become more important to you with every reading.

Another easy transition toward a daily habit is to spend 30 days reading the 30 chapters of Proverbs in the Old Testament. If the calendar says it's the 16th day of the month, turn to Proverbs 16 and explore God's words there. If it's the third day of the month, read Proverbs 3. Like the book of James, the meaning of the scripture transforms as you pass through the various seasons of your life. You'll never be disappointed in the messages you take from a chapter in Proverbs.

9. PUT OTHERS BEFORE YOURSELF

A foundational tenet of a spiritual vision involves putting the needs of others ahead of your own. "God is first. Others are second. I am third." It's easy for most of us to understand that God is first, but it can be more difficult to put others ahead of our own self-interest.

What if we woke up each day and before our feet hit the floor, we asked God how he would like us to serve others that day? Imagine how our focus would shift if before entering the office or going into a supermarket, we paused for a moment and asked God how we might serve others in that place. The only way to truly serve God is by serving others.

10. BE PREPARED FOR SPIRITUAL WARFARE

I've noticed when I'm attempting to grow closer to God, Satan moves closer to me. When I'm trying my hardest to live the life I believe God wants me to live, the evil one is tugging at my ankles and playing on my weaknesses. His only aim is to suck me into an abyss of sin. During these times, the devil attacks my loved ones and threatens things that are important to me, hoping I'll retreat in fear. When battling Satan, we must be bold in our faith and remain confident that our all-powerful God stands beside us.

As men, we tend to be skeptical about many things. Most of us operate within the framework of "seeing is believing." If it sounds too outrageous to be true, we hold our familiar position: We won't believe it until we see it. In the hidden dimensions of the spiritual realm, waiting for proof is not a luxury we get to enjoy. Christians understand that faith in an unseen God is essential. A similar sort of intuition warns us that Satan exists, and that spiritual warfare is real. The enemy may be invisible, but he is a real threat to our lives and our relationship with Christ.

Satan will use every enticement to lure us away from God. To avoid falling prey to his tactics, we must first acknowledge that the threat is real and then educate ourselves about the battle. Since the Garden of Eden, man has wrestled with the war between flesh and spirit. Satan capitalizes on our weakness for the flesh and uses pornography, lust and adultery to destroy our lives. As men, we resort to avoidance and denial as coping mechanisms when Satan exploits our weaknesses, but God calls on us to be intentional in our efforts to understand and overcome the devil's work.
Once you accept that spiritual warfare is real and begin to recognize the work of the evil one, you can take solace in the words from Matthew 28:18-20.

> *Then Jesus came to them and said, "All authority in heaven and on earth has been given to me. Therefore, go and make disciples of all nations, baptizing them in the name of the Father and of the Son and of the Holy Spirit, and teaching them to obey everything I have commanded you. And surely I am with you always, to the very end of the age."* **MATTHEW 28:18-20 NIV**

We were given all we need to be victorious over Satan when Christ died to conquer sin. We can take comfort in knowing that God looms large. He is in charge. Amen!

11. AVOID THE VAMPIRES

I once had a leadership expert tell me that the typical workplace is made up of two distinctly different types of employees: vampires and unicorns. The vampires are a negative force that drains energy and enthusiasm from everyone around them. These employees are miserable in their work circumstances and want everyone else to be equally miserable. Unicorns, on the other hand, fart sunshine no matter what happens. They love everything about their jobs, and they love everyone they work with. Either extreme is bound to cause some level of dysfunction in the workplace.

When you implement the components of a spiritual vision for your life, watch out for vampires. The people with whom you are most closely connected will inevitably rain on your newfound spiritual parade. It doesn't matter if that person has been your best friend since Cub Scouts. The minute he notices a change in your life's trajectory, he's going to have something to say that may discourage you. When this happens, know that the concern has more to do with him than you. His underlying issue could be a fear that you no longer have room for him in your life. Others will be jealous because you have gained a peace that they do not know how to achieve.

You don't have to look for a happy herd of unicorn buddies. Just be aware that some people won't support your decision to pursue a purpose-filled life that is pleasing to God.

Once you have your spiritual vision in place, make it your goal to bring your friends around to your new way of thinking. Don't be surprised if they call you out when your thoughts or actions don't match your new vision. It happens. Be consistent when you can and know that your actions will carry far more weight with skeptics than your words.

12. BEGIN WITH THE END IN MIND

You might ask yourself what God wants you to do with the rest of your life. Spoiler alert: God's vision for your life is that you become more like him with every passing day. It's that simple.

Once you've aligned your heart and mind around the idea of creating a spiritual vision, the real work begins. Along the way, you'll hit speed bumps that feel like real setbacks. You may come to a fork in the road where you face painfully tough choices. Don't be surprised when your spiritual quest runs out of gas. When your needle is on empty, turn to God and ask him for encouragement and the resilience to fuel your journey. God is a flawless navigator, and he will be with you for every mile of the journey.

Now It's Time To Get To Work

Now that you know where you're going, it's time to lay out the map for your journey. As with any worthwhile plan, you must spend time creating a mission statement, identifying the core values that will guide your actions, and identifying the specific steps that will get you closer to your goal.

Put your plan in writing. Plans that don't get written down tend to meander off course or abruptly end. Set aside time each day to review your plan. Is there forward motion? Once you have a clearly defined a written plan for your spiritual vision, you'll be on your way to a life truly worth living.

CHAPTER ELEVEN

11

Sharing Your Story

Sharing your Christian testimony is a powerful way to build community, make a personal connection with other men and demonstrate God's work in your life. Our testimonies, whether they recount our stories of salvation, gratitude or hardship, reflect the uniqueness of our personal journeys and illustrate God's workmanship. Our stories are at the heart of Christian life. Scripture emphasizes the importance of telling our stories to reveal God's work in us. Through sharing our stories, we honor our own experiences, trials and triumphs, while fulfilling the call to serve as ambassadors for Christ.

Depending on your life's circumstances and where you are in your Christian journey, there are at least three different ways to structure your story. The Salvation Testimony reveals how God saved you, transformed your life and provided a new purpose. The Praise Report recognizes and celebrates the blessings and good works God has accomplished for you and through you, reinforcing your faith and encouraging others by letting them know the same opportunities exist for them. Lastly, the Hardship Testimony shows others the depth of your struggles and disappointments but demonstrates how faith can sustain them during challenging times. Each style of testimony serves the purpose of motivating, inspiring and instilling hope.

REASONS TO SHARE YOUR TESTIMONY

There are many important reasons to share our personal stories. Throughout the Bible, we find examples of the transformative power that comes from sharing the good news of Christ. There are references where Jesus commands new believers to share what God has done in their lives. In Luke 8:26-39, Jesus told the demon-possessed man he healed in Geransenes, to go and share what God had done for him. Our testimonies can plant seeds of revival, repentance and salvation, as illustrated in John 4:4-38, where Jesus meets the Samaritan woman at the well. Per his instruction, she went back to her village and told people of her encounter, which led many to believe in Christ. The passage found in Revelation 12:11 reminds us that our testimonies empower others to overcome the enemy, affirming that our struggles can become victories through God's grace. Sharing our experiences brings glory to God by acknowledging his work in our lives.

> *"We are therefore Christ's ambassadors, as though God were making his appeal through us. We implore you on Christ's behalf: Be reconciled to God. God made him who had no sin to be sin for us, so that in him we might become the righteousness of God."* 2 CORINTHIANS 5:20-21

As God's ambassadors, our stories illuminate the character of Christ and show that our lives exemplify Christ's teachings, influencing those around us even before we begin to speak.

"Be wise in the way you act toward outsiders; make the most of every opportunity. Let your conversation be always full of grace, seasoned with salt, so that you may know how to answer everyone." COLOSSIANS 4:5-6

TELLING YOUR STORY

You'll find that identifying your life's milestones can be a great place to start with your testimony. Once you've mapped out the chronological timeline of your life, note as many details as possible, allowing your narrative to flow naturally. Keep your story concise, concentrating on the core message while being relatable; the truths of our everyday moments will resonate deeply with others. Contemplative prayer is essential as you seek God's guidance for effectively communicating your experiences.

When sharing testimony, it's best to adopt a mindset of authenticity and vulnerability as you begin to lay out the relevant facts. While it may feel awkward at first, an attitude of vulnerability will foster a genuine connection with others. In our most raw and honest moments, we reveal our strengths and also the fears and uncertainties that have shaped us. Acknowledging that we don't have all the answers creates an environment of trust and encourages others to be candid about their journeys. Embracing vulnerability can lead to deeper relationships by breaking down barriers that invite understanding and mutual trust. Resist the temptation to embellish your story to make your life seem more interesting. Your story has been crafted in the perfection of God and that's as good as it gets.

STRUCTURING YOUR TESTIMONY

Try to map out your life in increments of five or ten years as you build a historical account. Make note of both the happiest and saddest days of your life. Try to remember the approximate dates of events that shaped your life. Reflecting on your most challenging experiences and the times you've profoundly felt God's presence will help you demonstrate how God has changed you. Describe the emotions and circumstances that surrounded these milestones. These steps will give you clarity about your past and help you frame your story in a compelling way that draws attention to God's transformative power.

Now that you've done the real work, add structure to your testimony by answering the following questions:

1. What was your life like before you discovered a personal relationship with Jesus Christ?
2. What events or people most influenced your journey to faith?
3. How has God transformed your life since you came to know him?
4. How do you believe God is using you today to grow his kingdom?

Do your best to tell your story in seven minutes or less. There may be times when you can go into greater depth about the details of your journey, but we live in a fast-paced world and most people will only have a few minutes to hear what you have to say. Keep your message short, sweet and simple. Keep the main thing the main thing. The most important thing is to share that God changed a sinner like you and he can do the same for anyone else who chooses a relationship with him.

When you feel prompted to share your story, pray to God for guidance and confidence. Whether you're waiting in line at the hardware store or playing a round of golf with a stranger, God has put that person in that place at that specific time and in your presence for a reason. Seize the opportunity.

The real power of sharing our Christian testimonies is not just in the act itself, but also in the connection, healing and encouragement it enables. By telling our stories with humility and honesty, we plant seeds of faith in others.

www.ingramcontent.com/pod-product-compliance
Lightning Source LLC
Jackson TN
JSHW020511200225
79156JS00004B/10

* 9 7 9 8 9 9 2 5 0 8 6 1 1 *